To PAUL, I sincerely
most regards to hook!
Hope you enjoy Cheers,

31 AUG 96

Sled Driver

Flying the World's Fastest Jet

Third Edition

by
Brian Shul

MACH 1, Inc.
Chico, California

MACH 1, Inc.
PO Box 7360, Chico, CA 95927

Library of Congress Catalog Card Number: 91–062709

ISBN: 0–929823–08–7

First printing, 1991

Printed in Singapore by Craft Print Pte, Ltd.

This book is for my parents, who encouraged and supported my desire to fly, and waited patiently for twenty years until I was through.

Acknowledgments

My grateful thanks to the following people who helped me in a variety of ways to create this book: Colonels Nevin Cunningham and Tom Alison for their permission to photograph the jet in its local habitat; Major Benny Dennis for his superb airmanship in the T-38 who could always "put me there" for the picture; Sergeant "Ange" Strickland for Pace Chase coordination; Bill Witzke, George Hall and Bob Townsend for their expertise, encouragement and friendship; Master Sergeant Mike Haggerty, Ferrari Color Lab, and Katie Bowles in assisting with photographic slides; Fran Crawford and Mike Connors for their time in proof reading; Captain Ed "Otto" Pernotto, a veritable encyclopedia of military knowledge and good friend; Paul Farsai for taking a chance and keeping the faith; Lieutenant Colonel Walt Watson for gracious consent to use his name and for being there; Janet and Elsie for taking care of all their "boys"; and a loving thanks to Sheila O'Grady, without whose talents and perseverance this book could not have happened.

Contents

Preface 13

Introduction 15

CHAPTER I **First Meeting** 19
    The Interview 19
    Day Four 20
    Interview Sim 26

CHAPTER II **In Preparation** 28
    The Guy in Back 28
    In the Box 30
    In Thrust We Trust 34

CHAPTER III **Training Flights** 36
    The "B" 36
    Preflight 38
    Suit Up 39
    The Launch 43
    Aerial Refueling 54
    The Accel 59
    The Deep Blue 65
    Systems 69
    The Suit 71
    Night 74
    Recovery 76

CHAPTER IV Going Operational 84

    Supporting Cast 88

    Weather 92

    En Route 100

    The Unpredictable 104

    MIG Runner 106

    The Return 108

    "The High Untrespassed Sanctity of Space…" 113

        East 113

        West 113

    A Crew Finishes 117

CHAPTER V Companion Trainer 119

    Pace Chase 119

CHAPTER VI On Display 123

    The Rare Show 129

CHAPTER VII The Legacy 135

    Final Roar 141

    Photography Notes 146

Preface

We at Mach 1 have maintained our position for the past five years as the world's leading publisher of unique and high quality aviation prints and calendars. Our commitment to excellence has been exemplified by working with only the most accomplished aviation photographers in the world.

We first met Brian Shul two years ago after being exposed to his exceptional SR-71 photos. It was then that we began to learn more about the man behind the images. Upon meeting him, we began to realize his love for photography was only exceeded by his love for life itself. Here was a man who had been told he would never fly again after a near-fatal crash in the jungle of Southeast Asia, yet he went on to become an inspiration to many.

When learning of his ability to bring his experience to life through words, it was only natural that we combine his two talents of photography and writing, and create this one-of-a-kind book. We are proud to bring to our readers this work of love and passion so eloquently expressed on the following pages.

We hope you too, will be inspired by both his outstanding photography and his experience as an SR-71 pilot.

— Paul P. Farsai —
Mach 1, Inc.

Introduction

In 1966, I was still in high school. That same year the SR-71 Blackbird was already being brought on line in the U.S. Air Force inventory. For the next quarter of a century, this unique aircraft roamed the globe performing its role as an intelligence gathering platform for the United States. When it was first introduced into service, it was the fastest, highest flying air-breathing jet the world had ever seen. When it retired in 1990, the same could still be said.

Working in secrecy, chief SR-71 designer Kelly Johnson, and his team of experts built an airplane in the 1960s that both mystified and impressed the aviation world. The end product showed what could be achieved when talent and dedicated effort were not impeded by constant budgetary constraints. The SR-71 represents the blending of engineering genius, the willingness to break new ground, and superb project management. It was impossible to be associated with this aircraft and not feel the intense pride and dedication which went into every aspect of its construction.

My association with this aircraft, and subsequent love for it, occurred late in the plane's military life. In 1983 I came to Beale Air Force Base, California ready to begin training in a jet I had long considered out of my reach. I knew it was the world's fastest plane, but that didn't begin to really describe this black machine, this sensuous design of blended metals and elegant lines. The SR-71 had a lure for pilots all its own; it had an exciting combination of grace, speed, and danger. It was affectionately called "The Sled" by those who flew it. Here was a plane with a mission, and the heart to perform it with impunity.

This is not a story of the making of the SR-71, nor is it a technical digest of the many intriguing facts and figures about the plane. (For a comprehensive book detailing its history and capabilities, I highly recommend *Blackbird*, by Paul F. Crickmore, Osprey Publishing Limited, 1986.) Instead, this book is one man's view of what it was like to fly the world's fastest jet. I never imagined I would someday fly the SR-71. It was yet another exciting chapter in a life already blessed with many rewarding experiences.

This is a love story too, because I could not fly this airplane and not love it. I have purposely avoided certain specifics throughout the text, because they are not the focus of this story. The reader won't find secrets revealed in this book. Someday, someone will declassify bits of information about this jet, publish them, and then it won't matter to anyone anymore. I could never write that book. As one who shared intimate secrets with the airplane, I feel less inclined to reveal all that she could do. Most of the men who flew her feel the same way. To fly this jet, and fly it well, meant establishing a personal relationship with a fusion of titanium, fuel, stick and throttles. It meant feeling the airplane came alive and had a personality all her own. To betray her confidences now would be unthinkable.

My experiences and those of my back-seater are no more and no less than those of many other men who strapped themselves into this black aircraft. Our experiences were more typical than exceptional of the many who went before us and the few who flew the jet after us. My back-seater and I were always grateful for the opportunity to serve our country in this particular way.

Few aviators ever got the chance to fly the SR-71. In over twenty years of service, a total of only 314 Air Force aviators flew the Blackbird. (In the same time period over 6,000 Air Force aviators flew the F-4 Phantom II.) I was one of only 152 Air Force pilots to fly the SR-71 during its lifetime. The following pages describe a little of what that was like.

The cockpit was my office. It was a place where I experienced many emotions and learned many lessons. It was a place of work, but also a keeper of dreams. It was a place of deadly serious encounters, yet there I discovered much about life. I learned about joy and sorrow, pride and humility, and fear, and overcoming fear. I saw much from that office that most people would never see. At times it terrified me, yet I could always feel at home there. It was my place, at that time in space, and the jet was mine for those moments. Though it was a place where I could quickly die, the cockpit was a place where I truly lived.

SR-71, SR, Blackbird, HABU, Lady in Black, The Jet . . . **Sled**

CHAPTER I

First Meeting

When I was a boy, I built a plastic model of the SR-71. It was not my favorite model. It was big and fit awkwardly among my other models of fighter jets. It didn't come equipped with menacing looking rockets or bombs that I could paint and hang from the wings. Finally, the black color made the excessive glue, which I had so ardently applied, all the more obvious as it oozed along the seam of the fuselage. As I studied the finished product, I wasn't impressed.

Many years later, I found myself standing proudly next to my fighter jet at the Cleveland National Airshow. I had flown a demonstration flight earlier in the day, and I enjoyed talking with the crowd around my plane. While I stood there, I heard the public address system announce that the SR-71 would arrive in a few minutes to make a low pass. I had always wanted to see this strange aircraft in person, so I perched myself on top of my jet for a better view. I was a fighter pilot in the Tactical Air Command (TAC), and didn't want anyone to think I was too interested in a Strategic Air Command (SAC) aircraft. The SR-71 was from SAC where most airplanes were big and non-maneuverable. The SR-71, though, was the world's fastest jet, and pilots do respect speed, so I watched.

It arrived precisely on time. As the black aircraft grew closer, I noticed it was pointed on every end. It had a sinister look that suggested more than just cameras were carried on board. When it reached show center, the pilot pushed his throttles to maximum power. From half a mile away, the sound vibrated the open canopy I was grasping. Two long plumes of flame extended symmetrically from the rear of the black jet. Its nose pointed upward 45 degrees from the horizon as it started a steep climb. Then this aircraft, closer in size to a Boeing 727 than a fighter, accelerated effortlessly until, in moments, it was a dot. I was impressed.

THE INTERVIEW

The 9th Strategic Reconnaissance Wing (9th SRW) carefully selected its SR-71 pilots. Each volunteer for this special duty submitted an information package to the 1st Strategic Reconnaissance Squadron (1st SRS), where it was thoroughly evaluated. To be competitive, a pilot needed a high level of flying experience in jet aircraft, an excellent record, and the endorsement of his commander. If the squadron were interested, it arranged a one week interview at Beale Air Force Base with the applicant. Beale, located near Marysville, California, was the home of the SR-71 and the only base where training was conducted. I was excited when I learned I would get an interview. I wasn't even sure if this were the kind of flying I could do, but I was eager to find out.

The interview was a well-organized week of activities designed to evaluate the candidate, and in turn, enabled the candidate to evaluate his own desire to join the program. Flying the SR-71 wasn't a job for every pilot. During the first two days of the interview, the pilot applicant completed an astronaut physical. The afternoon of day three, he spent in the SR-71 simulator getting familiar with the cockpit and learning more about the mission of worldwide reconnaissance. Getting a close look at the jet and observing a launch were scheduled for the fourth day. The final day the applicant spent at the 1st SRS, meeting squadron members and talking flying. By this point, the applicant knew if this business were for him or not. For me, the first two days were easy, the third challenging and the fifth a pleasure. Of the five days, the fourth day stood apart from all the rest.

If I were going to fly this aircraft, I wanted to touch it and inspect it personally. Seeing the jet up close was essential, much like a concert pianist inspecting the piano before the concert. The turning point of my interview week and the moment when I made my decision to fly the SR-71 occurred on the afternoon of day four when I got to see the jet.

DAY FOUR

The 1st SRS Operations Officer escorted me out to the hangar area to observe an SR-71 launch. The launch included the engine start, taxi and takeoff. We arrived early, and walked to an adjacent hangar to look at another SR-71 up close. Inside the hangar, there were no sounds of drills turning, compressors whining, or men shouting. Instead of the normal din encountered in this place of work, the hangar was silent. As the black jet sat ominously before me, I felt more as if I were in a museum than a hangar. The aircraft was bigger than I had imagined; it was long in body. I instinctively looked toward the front cockpit. It sat well forward of the wings and engines, as if at the tip of a long sword.

Only with a feeling closely resembling reverence could I approach this sinister looking champion of speed.

The skin of the aircraft was rough, resembling a fine grade of sandpaper in places. Other parts of its body felt like smooth plastic. I began to realize that titanium did not cover every surface of the aircraft. The exterior was surprisingly irregular for an airplane built for speed; it had many grooves and expansion joints. The actual skin of the aircraft made up the shell of the fuel tanks. There were no bladders inside these fuel storage areas. Instead, as the aircraft reached its cruising speed and heated up, the skin expanded and tightly sealed the fuel inside the airplane. On the ground, fuel seeped through numerous joints and seams along the aircraft creating pools of fuel (JP-7) on the hangar floor. It was messy, but not a fire hazard since JP-7 did not ignite easily. As I stood there near the mess of fluids oozing from the seams of the aircraft, I realized how closely the real SR-71 resembled the glue stained model I had built as a boy.

The flared edge of the fuselage, called the chine, curved back gracefully into the wings, creating a lifting body that helped reduce fuel consumption at high speeds. I closely inspected this beast with a mixture of awe and respect and realized the Blackbird was more than an assembly of aircraft parts; it had a strong presence, more powerful than any airplane I had ever known. I studied the spikes: the large black cones leading into the engine intakes. Their tips were sharp to the touch. I understood little about their function, only that they were part of an advanced inlet design. The immense engines alluded to speeds above Mach 3. (Mach 1 equals the speed of sound.)

Looking up into the back end of the jet, I noticed the huge afterburner (AB) sections of the J-58 engines. Most fighter jets have afterburners. It is an extended section of the engine that produces augmented thrust beyond normal 100 percent military power. The normal throttle range is from idle power to military power. The throttles then slide over a detent to engage the afterburner. The afterburner range goes from minimum to maximum afterburner, or min AB to max AB. When the pilot selects afterburner, raw fuel is dumped into the burner section of the engine. When the fuel ignites, the afterburner lights off, giving the aircraft a surge of power. Depending on the size of the engine, a long flame extends from the tail end. I began to wonder what full AB would feel like in this jet, from a cockpit located 100 feet forward of the engines. I also wondered if I would ever think flying three times the speed of sound as routine. I left that quiet hangar and felt a nervous anticipation as I imagined piloting this beast. The crew had arrived in their support van at a nearby hangar, and it was time to watch an SR-71 launch.

The sights and sounds of the start sequence resembled a combination of a NASA space launch and a Daytona 500 pit crew in action. The start cart used to turn the main

The Buick V-8 Start Cart.

Tetraethyl Borane ignites JP-7 and with a
burst of flame an SR-71 engine is started.

engine shaft consisted of two Buick V-8 automobile engines in tandem. A chemical agent called Tetraethyl Borane (TEB), was used to ignite the fuel during engine start and whenever afterburner was selected. Because of the extreme temperatures experienced at high speeds, the fuel was designed to resist ignition under normal conditions. As the J-58 engine spooled up, the pilot signaled he was going to start the number one engine. Easing the throttle to the idle setting caused the TEB to hit the combustion chamber of the engine and an emerald green flame burst out of the burner section. The J-58 reached idle power amidst the noise of the screaming Buicks. The sound of floored V-8s seemed out of place next to this futuristic-looking flying machine. The uproar reached its climax as the Buick V-8s reached their top RPM and the engine stabilized in idle. This sequence was repeated for the number two engine. After both engines were started, the start cart wound down and the steady pitch of idling J-58s superseded all other sounds. This controlled chaos was normal start procedure for every flight.

While many people scurried beneath and around the Blackbird, I was escorted to a radio-equipped blue car that was always present when an SR-71 taxied. SR-71 crews referred to this vehicle as the mobile car. Able to communicate with the crew of the aircraft and other agencies, the mobile crew — one pilot and one Reconnaissance Systems Officer (RSO) — could offer assistance when necessary and help coordinate flight changes. The mobile also scanned the taxiways and runway for any debris or objects that could present a hazard to the SR-71. The mobile crew removed anything larger than the size of a dime found in the path of the jet. With nitrogen filled tires riding at 400 psi, the SR-71 could easily blow a tire if it rolled over any hard objects.

The jet taxied out with an entourage of vehicles: maintenance trucks, the physiological support van and the mobile car. Prior to takeoff, the pilot performed an engine run in a designated area near the runway.

I watched and listened as the pilot ran each engine up to military power and checked the RPM and temperatures to insure all was well. At 30,000 pounds of thrust, only one engine was run up to military power at a time. The jet's exhaust kicked up a whirlwind of dust and debris behind the run up area. The sound of the engines set this day apart. The gutty roar of the J-58s grabbed my insides and tugged at me. This engine sound was born from 1950s technology and was a trademark of the Century Series fighters I was born too late to fly. The older jets were loud, big, and built solidly. New technology emerged in the 1970s and I had flown aircraft with the newer fan jets. These engines were more fuel efficient but they didn't sound the same, nor were they

In the run-up area, a Sled waits for takeoff.

On takeoff roll, the Sled roared in full afterburner like no other.

as rugged. The SR-71 stood before me as something out of the past. It had all the defiance and pride of the older jets, the kind that had made a 10-year-old boy in 1958 want to fly. As this sound penetrated my ears, I again felt that same desire. I worried little now about space suit discomfort or what affect this assignment would have on my career or my personal life. The Blackbird was talking to me and I was listening.

I stood halfway down the runway to watch the takeoff. The pilot lit the afterburners and I heard two distinct booms that sounded like cannons in the distance. As the jet passed me, the thunderous, piercing sound of the engines at maximum power was not so much heard as it was felt. The sound vibrated my body and reached in and grabbed my soul. It had me. Here was a jet built long ago, still flying the same mission for which it had been designed. It could go places other airplanes couldn't, and bring back intelligence information vital to our nation. It was playing for keeps and still winning. I wanted to be a part of it.

INTERVIEW SIM

Day four of the interview had been the most inspiring, but day three had been the most challenging. It consisted of a familiarization and evaluation in the SR-71 simulator (sim). A one hour briefing preceded the simulator session. An SR-71 instructor pilot (IP) reviewed a wealth of information about the switches, levers, and gauges in the cockpit. As I gazed intently at the cockpit drawings and tried to absorb my instructor's words, I found myself filled with wonder at glimpsing at the inside of an aircraft that had been so secret for so long.

Armed with my sparse knowledge of cockpit switchology, I climbed into the SR-71 simulator. The IP was going to evaluate my flying skills, or so I thought. He was actually going to test my stress capacity. Even with the previous hour's instruction, I felt unprepared to properly fly this sim, but I wasn't going to let him know that. Everyone wanted to look good, and fighter pilots would rather die than look bad. I was about to die.

With a death grip on the stick and eyes scanning frantically across a hostile instrument panel, I devoted half my strength to appearing unflustered and in control. The IP baited me with easy maneuvers and I gained an artificial sense of confidence. He told me I was doing well and asked if I would like to try Mach 3 speed. Already overloaded, I uttered a weak response and hoped it sounded positive. Again the instructor gave me an easy scenario and I found it a bit surreal to see the

Mach indicator read '3.' Throughout it all, the instructor questioned me, testing my recall and adaptability to a new cockpit. The stress level mounted. I was told I was doing well at Mach 3. As I was gaining some confidence, I was asked if I would like to try to maintain Mach 3 flight without the aid of the stability augmentation system (SAS). Most high performance aircraft have this system, and normally it is never turned off in flight. The SAS helps jets remain stable at break-neck speeds. My instructor assured me it was quite all right. As I turned the SAS off I thought, "These guys must be terrific pilots to fly like this!" I maintained control for three seconds, then the sim died. With a disheartening "thud" all gauges stopped functioning and the lights flickered off. With both hands clutching the stick, I stared blankly at frozen cockpit instruments. In a grave tone, my instructor announced I had broken the simulator. "My God," I thought, "they trusted me with all this secret information and I broke the million dollar sim!" With a long face and more shaking of his head, my instructor quietly asked me to get out of the sim and added he was doubtful if they could fix it anytime soon. All present agreed they had never seen anyone do anything like this before. I was barely able to walk. Drenched in sweat, I retreated to the cold silence of the briefing room. I sat there feeling a lot like the kid who just wrecked Dad's car. While I was imagining my instructor and the sim technicians discussing my lack of flying ability, they were, in fact, having quite a chuckle. This was all part of the stress test. Years later the same instructor confided in me that I had done very well in that phase of the interview, and he had strongly endorsed my selection for training.

CHAPTER II

In Preparation

THE GUY IN BACK

The SR-71 carried a crew of two although some days it seemed like the crew carried the airplane. The man in front was the pilot and did all the flying. The man sitting four feet behind the pilot wore the wings of an Air Force navigator and was the RSO. He managed the sophisticated navigation and sensor equipment, but his duties went far beyond navigating and activating cameras. He handled the electronic defensive systems, operated four radios continuously, and was a flight engineer when the pilot needed a problem resolved. There were days, too, when he was a cheerleader and a coach. How well the guy in back (GIB) balanced these tasks directly affected the mission.

There was a distinct division of duties between cockpits, but the nature of the jet and its mission required a coordinated effort by the crew in all phases of operations. Pilot and RSO were paired at the start of training and remained a crew throughout their tour, normally flying only with each other. I got to know my RSO very well. I was lucky; not only was he extremely competent, he was a good friend, too. Most pilots felt this way about their RSOs. To me, my back-seater was the best RSO in the squadron, and it was a privilege to fly with him. His name was Walt Watson, and he was the only black man ever assigned to fly the SR-71.

I always felt a little sorry for Walt because he couldn't see much from the back seat. His head was normally down while he performed a multitude of tasks. His job satisfaction came from performing his mission well and getting the pictures. Sometimes we didn't understand what the other was going through, but we always depended on each other. During four years of sharing a myriad of emotions with the jet and each other, we formed a bond of mutual respect and friendship that will last the rest of our lives. Walt used to say that we lasted longer together than most marriages.

A crew is formed: Brian and Walter, the fighter pilot and the engineer.

It was a two-man airplane. A large part of the training was devoted to teaching us how to fly in concert from two completely different cockpits.

It took close to eleven months to complete training in the SR-71. While the second half of training was mostly flying the jet and accruing flight hours, the first half of training was torturous because of the many hours spent in the simulator. My RSO informed me he enjoyed simulator sessions as much as he enjoyed root canal work.

Flying an aircraft close to the edge of its performance envelope meant things got scary in a hurry when even the slightest malfunction occurred. Simulator training gave Sled crews experience with nearly every type of malfunction before it happened to them in actual flight. Although everyone agreed with this objective, it was hell stumbling our way through the learning process. The sweat-soaked-blank-stare-at-a-dying-instrument-panel look, introduced during the interview sim, was relived often.

Most crews were senior Captains or Majors with ten years flying experience. They were selected to fly the SR-71 because they were experienced and they were good. They didn't feel either during many days in the sim. At their former units they were all accustomed to being the top performers. It wasn't an easy process to watch both engine temperatures and pilots' egos reach breaking points during stressful moments in the sim. Everyone was humbled in the sim, or the box, as it was commonly called.

With a small number of crews on station at any one time, we would administer simulator sessions to others when our training was completed. Supervising sims was a two-man job. An instructor RSO sat at a large console equipped with the readouts of the back-seater's cockpit instruments. The instructor pilot sat directly behind the pilot, surrounded with a complete selection of switches designed to wreak havoc on aircraft systems and bring crews to their knees. The pilot and his instructor, and the RSO and his instructor, were in separate simulators and all four people communicated through headsets hooked into the intercom system.

The key to a successful simulator mission, indeed, the key to a successful aircraft mission, was clear and concise communication between the crew. Simple as this sounds, relaying information between cockpits with few similar gauges required some forethought. Communication became more critical when the sim was coming apart. During such emergencies, I needed to relay to my RSO the precise nature of the problem so he could read the necessary corrective steps from the proper checklist. As I struggled to identify the malfunction, critical seconds passed, creating additional problems. Many a hilarious utterance came forth from the front cockpit in the heat of a session, leaving the guy in back totally confused. One time I became so engrossed

There was much to learn, and the books couldn't leave the building.

A sim instructor reviews the route with his students. It will encompass the entire western United States — plenty of time for the instructor to create multiple emergencies.

The sim instructor reaches for 'fail' switches, insuring a miserable time for the guys in the box.

in describing indications to my RSO, my words became unintelligible. I had no clue why the sim was out of control. I pressed on undaunted with even more words, similar to raising my voice to a foreigner in hopes he will better understand my language. My instructor mercifully put the sim on freeze. I turned around and realized Walt had climbed out of his simulator cockpit and, along with my instructor, was peering over my shoulder. Totally frustrated, Walt asked to be shown the gauges with the new names.

The communication problem had to be solved. Walt and I spent hours sitting on the floor of his den, learning to speak to each other in shorthand about emergency procedures. This was no easy task. Walt was an engineer who wanted details; I was a fighter pilot who talked in adverbs. Eventually we got better and progressed well through the sim phase.

The turning point for us came when we did a simple thing that affected the rest of our days in the Blackbird. We had the sim to ourselves one day, and decided to show each other the details of what went on in the other man's cockpit. Walt eagerly put me in his seat, and for an hour he showed me all the RSO had to contend with. His workload was more overwhelming than I had thought. I then introduced him to the front seat and let him try driving for a while. He was exhausted. We got more from those few hours than any previous sim we had. We looked at each other's job differently and walked out of the simulator building with a new understanding of each other as professionals and friends. The thread of mutual respect woven that day enabled us to get through many trying flights later.

Not all of our training took place in the simulator. We learned about SR-71 systems in special classes with only the instructor, the pilot and the RSO in attendance. Only a few crews entered training each year, so academic classes were small. We learned fascinating things about the airplane. For example, JP-7 served not only as a fuel, but as a coolant and a hydraulic fluid as well. Some of the Blackbird's systems had to withstand extreme temperatures that resulted from high Mach. Fuel was routed around these systems to absorb heat and carry it away. The engine oil was thick like peanut butter before start, but then flowed smoothly when heated up. The jet expanded three to four inches under the heat of sustained high speed. Joints were designed into the airplane to accommodate this expansion in flight. Under normal temperatures on the ground, the jet leaked fuel profusely from these joints. Throughout our training, the jet's personality continued to grow as we learned more about the genius of its construction.

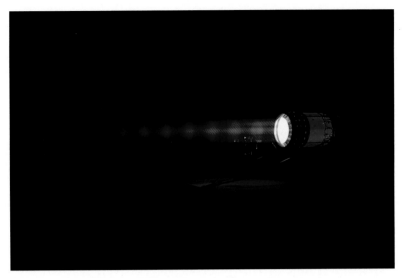

J-58 casing glows red from intense heat. Amazingly, moments after shutdown, the inside casing of the engine is cool to the touch.

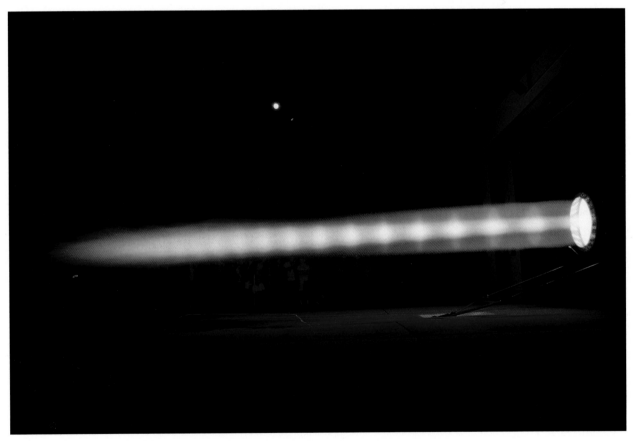

A night static engine run under a full moon.
The whole base will hear the full roar of the J-58.

Jet pilots have a personal relationship with their engines. In flight the engines were my legs. Engines keep pilots alive and bring them back from the fray. I was particularly interested in the SR-71's engines because they would take me out to the edge of where air breathing jets could operate, and sustain me there in the face of hostile threats. Two Pratt & Whitney JT11 D-20 engines powered the SR-71. The military designation for the power plant was simply J-58. Without its two J-58s, the Blackbird would never have been the thoroughbred it was. These engines supplied me with my only weapon: speed. I loved no part of this aircraft more.

I had a chance to view an engine up close before ever flying the jet. It was a brute. Built in the early 1960s, it was fashioned before the arrival of the lightweight metals of later years. Portions of the casing were molded with platinum and gold. Though slightly heavy by today's standards, it was an engine with heart that was built to last. I felt an increasing sense of confidence and awe about this mysterious jet; I wanted to feel those J-58s up at altitude where they belonged.

I had an opportunity to see the J-58 on a test stand during night engine runs. Few military bases invited base personnel to attend the viewing of engine runs. Beale was the exception to this practice, because the J-58 in full power provided a unique spectacle to the crowd. Although infrequent, this event always drew crowds. Word spread through the Wing and notices appeared on bulletin boards noting the scheduled date and time. No one was admitted without ear plugs. I witnessed several, and each time I enjoyed watching the uninitiated crowd push close to the safety line in anticipation of the engine start. As the engine was taken up to full power, I watched the spectators take several large steps backward in unison, with slight traces of fear and awe on their faces. The sound was beyond deafening. Standing fifty feet away, my entire body vibrated from the high decibel level. I remember feeling the buzzing vibration of my cheek bone as I raised a camera against it. One night after the run was over, an engine specialist took me over to the engine and put his hand on the inside of the casing, where moments before I had witnessed an intense flame. He was pointing out another engineering marvel of the SR-71; the ceramic lining in the afterburner section could withstand extreme temperatures then cool quickly.

Seeing the brute power displayed at the engine runs convinced me the airplane could sustain speeds of Mach 3 and beyond.

Full thrust on takeoff — a sight and sound long remembered, once heard.

"... charging off the runway in this jet was always exciting. I'd usually scare myself once in every five takeoffs. Well, maybe twice in five . . . ."

SLED PILOT

CHAPTER III

Training Flights

THE "B"

After six months of classroom academics and simulator training, it was time to be formally introduced to the Sled. For the pilot, the first few training sorties were flown in the SR-71B. This model of the SR-71 was modified with a raised rear cockpit, giving an instructor pilot enough forward visibility to safely fly and land the jet from the rear seat. The instructor pilot was an experienced crew member checked out to teach and evaluate others.

Generally, flying in the back seat of the B-model was not a fun experience. During landing, even with the raised seat, the high nose angle of the jet interfered with the IP's view of the runway. In addition, he had to operate the complex navigational system found only in the rear seat of the Blackbirds. Often, RSOs were seen giving IPs intensive briefings on back seat operations before B-model flights. The duties in back usually kept the IP so busy that the student pilot got most of the stick time.

Due to their high experience levels, squadron pilots had little trouble with learning to land and take off in the SR-71; the true value of the B-model was in teaching technique and proper position for aerial refueling. Aerial refuel was a necessity on every mission. If pilots couldn't learn this task, they wouldn't graduate from training. The simulator wasn't equipped with a visual display so refueling could only be properly taught in flight.

Despite the B-model's important role, pilots preferred flying the A. Flying the B meant one of two things and neither one was pleasant. First, the pilot could receive a checkride; a sortie flown with an evaluator in the back grading the pilot's performance. Second, the pilot could be the guy giving the checkride, so he'd be sitting in the cramped rear cockpit trying to understand systems he rarely saw. In either case, he flew without his RSO, with whom he was used to flying. Because there was only one B-model at Beale, after initial training we rarely had to fly it.

The B-model also served as the vehicle used by civilian and military dignitaries for orientation sorties. They came with a variety of reasons justifying a special flight.

The "B," the only Sled on the ramp attempting to disguise itself as something less than beautiful.

Often authority much higher than the squadron approved these sorties. The VIPs were familiarized with the cockpit in the simulator, got outfitted with space suits and helmets, and went out for the ride of their lives. B-model IPs really earned their pay when they took untrained civilians up on these flights. Afterwards, the VIPs received honorary patches and returned to their work places to claim momentary fame. They would never understand the deep personal attachment squadron members felt for the SR-71 or that many crew members silently resented their presence. Crews who flew the Sled had paid their dues through six months of strenuous training before their first flight. Crews often felt VIPs gained a flight without paying the price.

PREFLIGHT

The second half of the SR-71 training program was more to our liking than the first half since it consisted primarily of flying. We accumulated experience by flying the jet on training routes around the United States. After finishing with the B-model, it was nice to start flying with my RSO. Those first few flights made us appreciate our simulator training. The day before a mission, Walt and I looked over the maps and discussed the route. The next morning we received a weather briefing covering the mission. Since our flights covered large areas, we were well informed about the weather all across the country. Of primary concern was the weather in the refueling area and at primary divert bases. On long flights, we frequently returned to home base and found the weather completely different from the conditions in which we had left.

Following the weather briefing, we went to the Physiological Support Division (PSD) building. All the space suits were stored, checked, and repaired there. The building was also where we ate and dressed before being driven out to the jet. For years, crews were told to eat a high protein, low residue meal before flight. As more was learned about nutrition, people realized a continued diet of steak and eggs before flying wasn't healthy over a long period of time. Even so, the small dining facility at PSD still had steak and eggs as its main entree right up to the end of the SR-71 program. Other menu items were available, and each crew member learned, sometimes the hard way, what to eat and what not to eat before high altitude flights. As air pressure decreased at higher altitudes, gases inside our bodies expanded, so we stayed away from foods that produced intestinal gas. Like other phases of training, choosing what to eat was a learning process and everyone's body was different. I only ate a cheese omelet once. I thought I was going to give birth in the cockpit passing through 52,000 feet. I finally settled on peanut butter sandwiches; they seemed to work fine for me. We occasionally had visitors at PSD. One morning a small group of cadets joined Walt and me for our preflight meal. They ordered steak and eggs to keep with tradition. They looked bewildered as I hit the peanut butter and Walt dined on frosted flakes.

During the preflight meal, the crew chief came to our small dining room to brief us on any problems with the jet. We were also notified if our tankers were having any problems. The tankers were KC-135Q aircraft that were able to refuel the SR-71 in flight. They carried the JP-7 necessary for the fuel-thirsty Sled. If they weren't going to be there with the gas, we weren't going. About an hour and a half before takeoff time we went to the locker room to take a mini-physical and get dressed for flight. A technician took our temperature, blood pressure and insured we could clear our ears. If one of the crew was unable to fly, the mobile crew would fill in and fly the mission. In all the flights I observed, I never saw this happen. Scheduled crews rarely missed their turn in the Sled.

SUIT UP

Although the SR was configured so crews could fly without the space suit, we wore them on every flight. This procedure created a positive check of the aircraft's double oxygen system, and provided additional protection to the crew in case of ejection. Physiological Support Division technicians handled everything pertaining to the space suit. They helped the crews into their suits, ran all the checks, and then assisted the crews as they strapped into the cockpits. PSD personnel were experts on the effects of high altitude flight on the human body. Their personal assistance and expertise alleviated many potential problems in the cockpit.

The loss of cabin pressurization and nitrogen evolution in the body were two dangers that faced high altitude flyers. The space suit and cockpit protected us from these hazards. The ambient air pressure at high altitude is so low that unpressurized liquid evaporates in seconds. Without protection, human body fluids would boil away. At high altitude, the cockpit was pressurized to 25,000 feet. This meant that although the airplane might be flying at 75,000 feet, the cockpit would have the air pressure of 25,000 feet of altitude. The space suit provided backup protection if cabin pressurization failed at high altitude. If pressurization were lost, the space suit filled with air to provide the required air pressure on the body.

Another process happens at the low ambient pressure: nitrogen evolves from solid tissues into gas bubbles, usually near body joints. Sometimes the gas bubbles can slip

Wearing space suit and helmet, a crew member is well dressed for flight at altitudes where few go.

into the blood stream. This process is called the bends, and can be painful or even fatal. The space suit provided a closed environment in which crews could breathe 100% oxygen. Face plates were closed before takeoff, so by the time an SR-71 crew had finished aerial refueling, they had prebreathed pure oxygen for enough time to reduce the nitrogen in their bodies. Breathing pure oxygen all the time reduced the amount of nitrogen in the body, thereby reducing the opportunity for the bends to occur at high altitude.

Because we wore the suits for hours at a time, we were meticulous about putting them on. The space suit left us somewhat immobile, and we could no longer do things most people took for granted. With the suit on, we couldn't scratch our noses, brush hair out of our eyes, or adjust irritating folds in our undergarments. Through painful experience, I developed my own procedure for suiting up that prevented irritations from cropping up later. Underneath the space suit, we wore one hundred percent cotton longjohns, socks, and glove inserts. I made sure there were no creases in my longjohns, and I didn't wear the glove inserts. The SR stick was fat enough without having another layer of material between my hand and the stick.

After changing into the longjohns in the locker room, I went to the bathroom for the last time and walked into the next room where the PSD technicians had my space suit and helmet waiting. It was something like a rubber sweat suit, but heavier. I stepped into the rubber feet of the suit and rolled the suit up my legs. I carefully shook any wrinkles out. I slid my arms into the suit, and my head through the neck ring. A giant zipper, running up the center of my back, sealed me in the suit. Boots went on next, followed by gloves which clicked into metal rings at the ends of the arm sleeves. Before I put on my helmet, I stopped and took a deep breath. I knew my helmet was going to be on a long time before coming off again. With the helmet on, my head and neck had less freedom of movement. The weight of the suit seemed to gather at the ring around my neck, causing fatigue in the neck and shoulder muscles. The helmet weighed almost 12 pounds, and after a flight it was the first thing I wanted to take off. On one flight, an ear flap inside my helmet was folded over incorrectly. After the first refueling, I felt as if I was flying with a metal spike pounded into my left ear. Three and a half hours later I removed a helmet that had transformed itself into a torture device on my head.

Dehydration adversely affected our performance in the cockpit, so drinking fluids was an important task. To keep us going, PSD provided packaged food and drinks for consumption during our missions. Drinks were provided in plastic water bottles, and food was sealed in containers resembling toothpaste tubes. A long plastic straw extended from the end of the tube. It was similar to the sports bottles bicycle racers drink from during a race. By looking in the cockpit mirror, I could guide the long

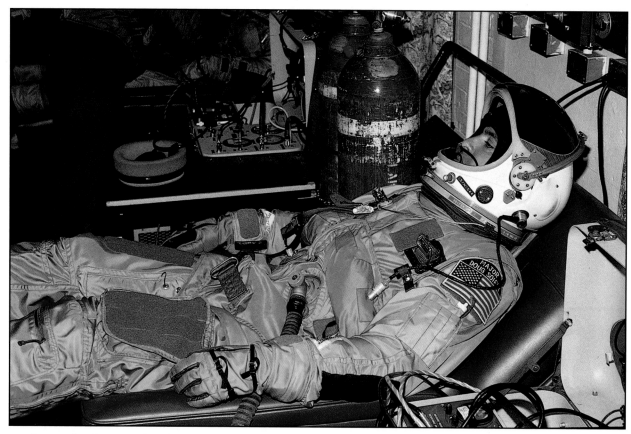

With suit checks completed, an RSO rests before getting on the van. Note plastic tube food straw in upper arm pocket. Velcro pads on knees secured thick checklists to legs.

Donning the helmet at PSD. It's got to fit right.

Pilot confers with mobile crew prior to strapping into cockpit.

straw to my mouth through a small opening, designed in the helmet for this purpose. Most crews took at least a water bottle. I normally carried a bottle of half water, half Gatorade. I tried the food once and decided I could do without it.

The suit was designed for sitting and could be comfortable once everything was on and adjusted properly. Most problems with comfort were best handled through prevention, and this meant attention to detail during suiting up. Techniques, discovered or passed on by others, helped make life more bearable in the suit. I learned I didn't have to adjust the rubber face seal, located in the helmet, as tight as the PSD folks insisted. I could also raise my face plate if needed, as long as I held my breath to prevent introducing nitrogen into my body. This was rarely done because of the potential danger of going unconscious from the lack of oxygen. The face plate was heated similar to rear window defoggers installed on many cars. This heat cleared the fog that formed from heavy breathing or the vapor left by an unexpected sneeze.

Often PSD allowed various groups of people to tour the facility and observe our routine. Walt and I have suited up in front of generals, military wives, and fourth graders, just to name a few. We got used to it and didn't allow the visitors to keep us from insuring everything was fitting just right. Sometimes we'd let the kids touch the space suit and they especially enjoyed seeing it inflate. Most people wanted their picture taken with this enigma of fasteners and hoses sitting in front of them.

Once I put my helmet on and sat in the van that would take us to the airplane, another phase of concentration began. I thought about the departure, the weather, and the rendezvous with the tanker.

THE LAUNCH

About an hour before takeoff, we would climb into the jet. The mobile crew had already set up the cockpits for us, and PSD technicians helped us through everything from climbing out of the van, to strapping us into the cockpit. They carried our water bottles, checklists, and flight manuals. After we climbed into the cockpit, we sat in our seats with our arms extended so the PSD technicians could reach all the connections in the cockpit. Two to three PSD folks expertly snapped, hooked, tugged, pushed and inserted parts of our suits to the life support systems. I often felt like the queen bee with devoted worker bees scurrying about me.

The cockpit environment was familiar; the sim had been a realistic representation of the aircraft. I expected the instrument panel to look worn from age, similar to other

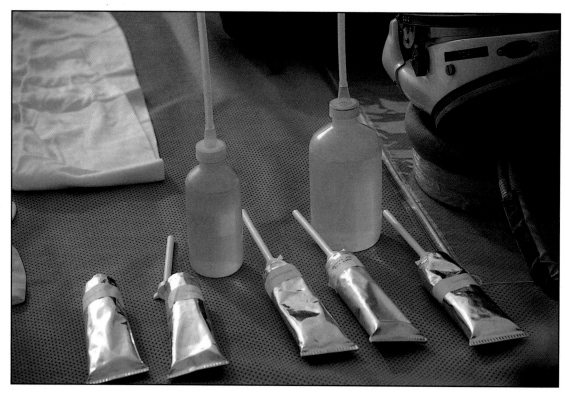

Tube food and water bottles await the crew.

Visitors were numerous and one never knew who would be watching the suit-up.

military jets I had flown. Normally, pilots did a walk-around inspection before climbing in the cockpit, and brought with them sweat, oil, and fuel on their gloves. Dirty gloves contributed to the deterioration of the cockpit and instruments. In contrast, SR-71 crews went directly from the van to the cockpit, skipping the walk-around. Specialists and the mobile crews performed the preflight inspections long before the flight crews arrived. Soiled hands rarely touched the SR-71's 20-year-old gauges. Clean space suit gloves worked in the SR-71 cockpit. Because of this, it looked newer than it actually was.

As good as the sim was, it couldn't prepare us for the sounds and the feel of the engine start. Even with the space suit and helmet on, the roar of the Buick V-8s winding up filled the cockpit. When the TEB exploded into the engine burner section, the jet awakened with a resounding thump I felt in the cockpit. I knew right away I had a tiger on a leash. Once in idle, a subtle vibration hummed through the jet which I could feel come up through the metal plates on the floor of the cockpit and into my boots. When all the pre-taxi checks were completed, the canopies were closed. It was a heavy canopy with a tight seal around the cockpit. Whenever it was shut around me, I felt entombed within a maze of dials, levers, and gauges.

While taxiing the aircraft, the pilot was continuously aware of the thrust generated by the J-58s. He kept the throttles in idle, and applied brakes to avoid overrunning the mobile car. The Sled always drew a crowd during the taxi to the runway. Even at Beale where it was a common sight, people stopped and watched the airplane roll past.

The engine run, from inside the cockpit, was nothing like listening to the overwhelming roar of the engines when standing outside. Inside the jet, it was relatively quiet. A solid vibration accompanied the hum of the finely tuned engines. Watching engine temperature gauges fluctuate radically, I always had faith in the J-58s because the readings quickly settled to within a few degrees of ideal.

When all the pre-takeoff checks were complete, maintenance personnel hammered the chocks out from under rock hard tires. The crew chief saluted with a thumbs up, and everyone moved away from the jet; it now was ready to take the runway. During the last few moments before takeoff, Walt and I said little to each other as we silently reviewed the takeoff and climb in our minds. On a sunny day I felt on top of the world knowing in moments many would watch, and even more would hear, our takeoff. We would soon be airborne gaining more valuable experience. In contrast, there were nights when I watched rain batter the windscreen and felt they didn't pay me enough to do this.

Amidst a host of PSD technicians, a pilot carefully lowers himself into his office.

Sled crew runs through pre-start checklist. Though separated by only a few feet, each man's personal experiences during the flight could be worlds apart.

The final closing of the canopy prior to taxi. On our first few flights, slight feelings of claustrophobia would occur when the heavy lid was sealed.

Sled taxies from hangar. Immediately, the Astro-Inertial Navigation System will begin tracking stars even in broad daylight.

Like royal attendants, numerous vehicles escorted the
Blackbird each time it taxied.

Flashing taxi light from SR-71 alerts mobile car that pilot is ready to taxi.

Number one for takeoff, a Sled driver sits behind thick
protective glass and prepares to take the runway.

Regardless of the weather or the mission, our concentration was high during takeoff. During this phase of flight, I felt the aircraft was competing with me to see who was in control. Normally, Walt and I flew with the intercom in the cold 'mic' position since continuously listening to the other guy breathing was bothersome. With the intercom button, or mic, in this position, we didn't hear the other guy unless we keyed the intercom button. If hot mic were selected, we could talk to each other without keying the intercom button. During takeoff we used hot mic to facilitate intercockpit communication in case of an emergency. With hot mic on, the RSO could usually tell by the pilot's increased rate of breathing if a malfunction were occurring. We were extra vigilant during takeoffs in this airplane. I had a theory that airplanes that crashed during landing were normally the result of pilot error. Airplanes that crashed on takeoff were usually caused by a sick airplane. I wanted to be ready if our airplane were going to be sick that day.

As the RSO counted down the seconds, I released brakes precisely for an on-time takeoff. Some pilots released brakes several seconds prior, to have the afterburners light right at takeoff time. This came under the heading of "style points" between the squadron pilots and mattered little to anyone else. Raising the throttles slightly and moving them past the military power detent, the afterburners ignited, then stabilized (hopefully). At this point the pilot pushed the throttles as far forward as possible, entering the maximum afterburner range. There was no doubt if the burners were engaged or not. When the afterburners lit, the acceleration was immediate. Both afterburners needed to light off within two to three seconds of each other or the aircraft would veer sideways from the power differential, and quickly end up in the grass. Normally, burner lights were not simultaneous, and I was rocked to one side of the cockpit, then the other, as each afterburner kicked in. With this kind of power, the takeoff roll was both short and fast. In less than 5000 feet we were airborne at 200 knots.

Immediately after takeoff, I reached for the landing gear handle. With the wheels extended, we couldn't go faster than 300 knots without exceeding the gear limiting speed. I promptly raised the gear to prevent this from happening. As the wheels were up and I passed the departure end of the runway, I already had between 350 and 400 knots. I gently pulled the nose skyward climbing in full afterburner. Because of the length of the forward fuselage, too abrupt a pull on the stick could result in overshooting the desired pitch angle. When this happened the momentum of the rising nose was difficult to arrest. While those on the ground were impressed with an extra steep climb, the pilot in the cockpit was even more astonished and was pushing forward on the stick with both hands. With a little practice, climb techniques were polished. Three minutes after I released brakes for takeoff, I was leveling the jet at

There was no doubt by the crew when the burners lit. It was like a swift kick in the pants.

Passing in a blur of furious sound, the pilot quickly retracts the wheels before starting climb after takeoff.

Climbing rapidly over the foothills of northern California, the SR-71 leveled at 25,000 feet in less than four minutes after takeoff.

25,000 feet. Normally, military jets performed full afterburner climb profiles only at airshows. We did them daily.

Once leveled off and out of afterburner, the jet flew much like a heavy fighter at subsonic speeds. The SR-71 normally launched with half a fuel load. A full load would have made it more difficult to abort the takeoff in case of emergency. Our first priority after takeoff, was to rendezvous with a tanker aircraft that would fill us with fuel for the route ahead.

AERIAL REFUELING

We normally refueled from our own fleet of KC-135Q tankers. These Q-models had been fitted with special ranging equipment that helped facilitate the rendezvous with the SR-71. My RSO and the tanker navigator electronically worked in concert to help bring two planes together at one preplanned spot in the vast expanse of sky. The tankers were always a welcome sight because of the Sled's appetite for fuel. It was imperative to get the gas. Routes were planned with little margin for error concerning fuel. If we were programmed for a full off-load of fuel from the tanker, and normally we were, we needed to get every drop.

I'd learned air-to-air refueling in two other airplanes, the A-7 and the A-10. Refueling the SR was similar procedurally, but it was difficult and more demanding. First, the forward visibility in the Sled was worse than what most pilots were used to. The triangular shape of the forward window did not compare to the bubble canopy of a fighter. Second, wearing a space helmet caused bothersome reflections, and limited my peripheral vision. Third, the SR-71 fuselage was long and the refueling receptacle was well aft of the cockpit. Because of this, we had to fly the jet slightly underneath the KC-135. This position was uncomfortable, and it didn't allow me to see much in the way of outside references. Using outside references meant finding things to look at on the tanker that told me I was in position. For example, in the A-10, the refueling receptacle was in the nose, so it was easy to watch the red, yellow, and green lines of the boom move in and out of its sleeve to tell us if we were in position. This system spoiled me because I didn't have to use the two rows of director lights on the underside of the tanker.

The director lights blinked signals to the receiver pilot, indicating his position relative to the tanker. One row of lights indicated vertical position, the other fore and aft. The lights worked automatically once the refueling boom was inserted into our aircraft. I had never used these lights before, but now flying further under a tanker than was comfortable, I depended on them. Just getting to the proper position so the tanker's boom operator could plug into my jet, was sometimes a chore. Initial attempts

Subsonic, a thirsty Blackbird seeks out its tanker.

Sled pilot eases the jet forward for crucial contact. When the Blackbird is in position, the tanker's boom operator will place the refueling nozzle into the SR-71's receptacle.

at refueling in the B-model were humbling. I soon learned if I lowered my seat, I could see everything much better. Even when it went smoothly, refueling in flight was extremely fatiguing for the pilot.

I was accustomed to being on the boom for just a few minutes to top off in fighters. In contrast, SR-71 refuelings took fifteen minutes or more which could seem like an eternity. This time was needed because the airplane took on an incredible amount of fuel. During a normal refueling we usually received over 11,000 gallons. This changed our gross weight by 70,000 pounds and caused a corresponding change in the center of gravity of our aircraft.

At the slow 300 knot range in which we were flying to refuel, the feel of the jet became sluggish as the SR filled with fuel. At these gross weights and slower airspeeds, the SR-71 became thrust limited during the last few minutes of refueling. In military power, we would start to fall off the boom. A disconnect was highly undesirable since the jet was less responsive now and to reconnect was more difficult. It also meant wasting time on the refueling track and this could affect our overall mission timing. The solution was to light one afterburner with careful finesse. The fine art of pulling the throttle ever so slightly up and just into the minimum burner range was handed down from one generation of SR pilots to the next. The SR is the only airplane I know that required the use of afterburner to stay on the boom.

Using one afterburner caused another problem: asymmetrical thrust. Some pilots used a little rudder to handle the yaw. Others left the rudders alone, flew sideways, and looked out the front quarter panel to see forward. The quarter panels were located on either side of the windshield. Only the left quarter panel was wired for defogging so we always lit the left burner to yaw right so we could use this feature if needed.

The most exciting moments on the refueling track were normally reserved for those final few minutes in afterburner on the boom with a very heavy jet. Once I selected min AB and the TEB dumped in, there was a pause, then the airplane lunged sideways and started to charge up the boom. With the left burner stabilized in min AB, I controlled our fore and aft position with right throttle. With this method, the pilot controlled the airplane by leading the power inputs. It was like flying a freight train because the airplane's inertia caused a lag between throttle input and aircraft response. It wasn't uncommon at this point for the director lights to resemble a pinball game, flashing from end to end as the fore and aft movements of the jet caused continual changes in relative position. I had to ignore the director lights, grit my teeth, and call on every bit of my experience to get to the end of the refueling track with a full tank.

Somewhere high above the wastelands of Nevada, contact is made, fuel is transferred, and a smile of satisfaction appears inside a space helmet.

Sled driver's view of approaching a KC-135Q. Director lights are visible on underside of tanker forward of wings. Dark rectangle near aft of tanker is boomer's window. Yellow line on tanker helped receivers line up with tanker, especially in bad weather.

Aerial refueling from the tanker boom operator's vantage point. The small ANS window on the Blackbird is visible just behind the rear cockpit.

Refueling was the most physically intense part of the entire flight for me. This was in direct contrast to my RSO's workload during refueling. I can remember hanging on the boom with a death grip on the stick, sweat in my eyes, turbulent weather, and one engine in burner. I asked my backseater how many minutes we had left on the track, hoping it would soon be over. Walt said he'd check in a moment as he was enjoying some butterscotch pudding tube food. I wanted to kill, but reserved myself for the four and a half excruciating minutes I had left on the boom. There really wasn't much Walt could do to help me on the boom except give me a countdown of fuel and time to completion. It was my baby, but Walt did help with encouraging words at times and mostly sat anxiously amidst the grunts and groans coming from the front seat.

Darkness, clouds, turbulence, a tanker without a functioning autopilot or a new boomer all contributed to making life difficult for Sled pilots in need of gas. Refueling was one of the phases of flight where everyone who flew the airplane had one or more humbling stories to tell. Some days the airplane just drove right in and hooked up, as easy as getting a drink at a drive-in. That so many refuelings were accomplished safely in the airplane was a tribute to the skills and experience level of the SR pilots who flew them. Even in the best of conditions, aerial refueling was always an intricate ballet of men and machines with little margin for error. Some days everything went right on the boom and I was an ace. Other days I thought someone had dumped a box of snakes in the cockpit and nothing went right. This vital procedure occurred two to four times each mission and made for many a sore arm at the end of the day.

THE ACCEL

After we got our fuel load, I eased the jet back, swung clear of the tanker and lit the burners. I felt myself pushed back into the seat as the afterburners lit off and the airplane accelerated forward. This was a comfortable feeling because we were heavy with fuel at dangerously slow airspeeds for the Sled. The tanker crews always enjoyed watching the SR accelerate past them. The SR was a drooling tiger off the leash, streaming fuel from full tanks, in full burner, blazing toward the unknown.

In full afterburners, we went into what we termed the dipsy maneuver. The dipsy maneuver was a gentle climb to just under 35,000 feet, followed by a gentle push on the stick, nosing the aircraft downhill to help it accelerate through Mach 1. We didn't want to bottom out below 30,000 feet because regulations didn't allow supersonic flight below this altitude in the continental United States. The pilot accomplished all this while the RSO obtained a clearance

Streaked with fuel, a satisfied Blackbird leaves the refueling track 65,000 pounds heavier than when it arrived.

An SR-71 clears a tanker and goes to full afterburners to build precious speed.

from Air Traffic Control, first to climb, and then to descend. Once the maneuver was started, it was hard to knock off. During training, the smoothness of our climb was in the hands of the FAA. We were another subsonic target on the air traffic controller's screen, flying at altitudes used by everyday commercial traffic. Sometimes air traffic controllers would not clear us to climb because of conflicting airline traffic. This was disconcerting as we were burning about one ton of fuel per minute in full power.

Once the jet was stable in a shallow dive, I engaged only partial autopilot controls because this maneuver was usually best when hand flown. We needed to push the airplane through the sound barrier before starting the climb. Because of its size and weight, the airplane always seemed to hesitate going faster than the speed of sound. It went supersonic with a heavy groan. Once there, it wanted to stay there. I began the climb at 450 knots and we were soon at Mach 1.1 with the airplane accelerating quickly. We reached Mach 2 swiftly, and the altimeter effortlessly wound up through 40,000 feet. This acceleration and climb required intense concentration because I had to check a multitude of things. My backseater helped by calling out checkpoints in the climb. Walt was also busy updating the navigation system and checking sensors because he was about to begin the meat of his mission.

As we passed through 50,000 feet, the sky began to turn a darker blue. I could spend little time enjoying the view though, as I was busy checking off speeds, altitudes, and temperatures. One of the most important jobs the pilot had was the monitoring of spike and door positions.

Large cones in the intakes, called spikes, controlled airflow into the SR-71's engines. The spikes, under computerized control, worked with the air bypass doors to help the engine operate at supersonic speeds. Aircraft travelling at supersonic speeds create a shock wave. Engines can't digest shock waves; if they try, flameouts occur. The inlet must slow air to subsonic speeds before it passes through the engine. The door vents, located on the engine housing just aft of the spikes, helped regulate the airflow in this process. The pilot manually operated the doors.

At higher Mach numbers, the spikes moved aft automatically as the airspeed increased. If needed, the pilot could take control of the spikes manually. The spikes controlled the shock waves at the threshold of the engine intakes. If a shock wave started moving back into the engine, the spike would push forward rapidly to relieve the aerodynamic disturbance. Whenever this occurred, the jet yawed violently with enough force to slam the pilot's head against the side of the cockpit. This put the jet in danger of going out of control, cost precious fuel to regain lost speed, and scared the hell out of both crew members. This aerodynamic disturbance was referred to as an unstart.

An SR-71 seeks out the deep blue.

Spike in the forward subsonic position. Forward and aft bypass vents are in view around shroud of engine. When this system malfunctioned, there was no greater headache for the crew.

An experienced pilot could sometimes hear the inlet duct rumble, which was an indication the shock wave was moving too far aft. With skillful manipulation of the air bypass doors, he could prevent an unstart. A newer digital inlet control system was fitted to the SR-71 in 1983, helping to reduce the overall number of unstarts. What is more important, this system programmed the spikes to move in unison when unstarts occurred, reducing the dangerous yaw movement of the aircraft at high Mach. When unstarts occurred, and they still did, the resulting yaw caused the nose of the jet to move violently sideways and pitch slightly upward. This upward pitch of the nose could spell doom for the crew. At 2000 miles per hour this maneuver could quickly become uncontrollable, causing the jet to break apart somewhere behind the cockpits. Several SR-71s were lost during development due to this phenomenon. The newer inlet control system worked better than the older analog system, and no jets with the new system installed were lost to unstarts.

The inlet system was the key to flying fast and sustaining that speed safely. It was also the one system a pilot had to master beyond question to fly the jet properly. Since this system was found on no other jet, it was a learning experience for every new pilot. In the process of accelerating, the pilot needed to change the position of the air doors with a small shifting lever. In the cockpit, gauges showed the precise position of the spike. Shifting at the proper moment was important. If he shifted too early the jet's acceleration was impeded by drag from excessive air venting overboard; if he shifted too late an unstart might occur. Every flight the pilot managed this roulette game that changed with different sets of atmospheric parameters. How and when the pilot shifted the air doors also depended on the airplane's personality. With few numbers of SR-71s flying, the pilot got to know each one intimately.

Pilots and RSOs experienced unstarts in different ways. The pilot was in control of pressing the edge of the engine's operating envelope. He had a better idea than the RSO of when and why the unstarts occurred. Unfortunately, the guy in back had neither gauges nor caution lights to warn him of an imminent unstart. The RSO may have his head down, running a diagnostic check one moment, only to find himself slammed into a corner of the cockpit amidst a flurry of checklists and maps, the next. It wasn't uncommon for the RSO to remind the pilot to shift conservatively during the acceleration. Some days, no matter what the pilot did, the jet was going to unstart. Managing the inlet system was a never ending series of adjustments by the inlet specialists on the ground, and the daily roulette game in flight.

It felt good to level off at altitudes where I knew I owned the sky. If all was working well, I could relax for a moment as I retarded the throttles slightly from the maximum burner position, to maintain the programmed Mach. Relax is a relative term; triple-sonic flight thirteen miles high requires unrelenting attention. After the stress of the takeoff, the refueling, and the acceleration, I always felt a sense of calm, once level in the steel blue sky.

The Blackbird loved being up high. She came into her own up there and never ceased to impress me with what she could do. Because of the design of the inlet system, the faster the jet flew the more efficient it became. Better range was attained by increasing the speed. This was the opposite of other jets I had flown, where fuel flow increased at higher speeds. Once the SR-71 was at cruise speed, I continually adjusted the throttles back to keep the speed down. The jet cruised in afterburner, but rarely was maximum power needed.

Our training flights took us over much of the western half of the United States. A typical sortie out of Beale included a rendezvous with a tanker over Nevada, accelerating to Mach 3 across Wyoming and leveling above 75,000 feet over Montana. We'd turn right approaching South Dakota, roll out in Colorado, and zip south to New Mexico. There we'd begin another right turn that would carry us through Arizona and straight to southern California, then out over the ocean and finally up to the Seattle area where we'd prepare to descend back to Marysville, California. This was a nice tour in two and a half hours.

To more fully understand the concept of Mach 3, imagine the speed of a bullet coming from a high powered hunting rifle. It is travelling at 3100 feet per second as it leaves the muzzle. The Sled would cruise easily at 3200 feet per second, with power to spare. There was a lot we couldn't do in the airplane, but we were the fastest guys on the block and frequently mentioned this fact to fellow aviators. I'll always remember a certain radio exchange that occurred one day as Walt and I were screaming across southern California 13 miles high. We were monitoring various radio transmissions from other aircraft as we entered Los Angeles Center's airspace. Though they didn't really control us, they did monitor our movement across their scope. I heard a Cessna ask for a readout of its groundspeed. "90 knots," Center replied. Moments later a Twin Beech required the same. "120 knots," Center answered. We weren't the

Workload in the cockpit was high, but an occasional glance outside was always rewarded with a memorable sight. Here author takes a look at the earth from 78,000 feet.

only one proud of our speed that day as almost instantly an F-18 smugly transmitted, "Ah, Center, Dusty 52 requests groundspeed readout." There was a slight pause. "525 knots on the ground, Dusty." Another silent pause. As I was thinking to myself how ripe a situation this was, I heard the familiar click of a radio transmission coming from my back-seater. It was at that precise moment I realized Walt and I had become a real crew, for we were both thinking in unison. "Center, Aspen 20, you got a ground speed readout for us?" There was a longer than normal pause. "Aspen, I show one thousand seven hundred and forty-two knots." No further inquiries were heard on that frequency.

When we flew at low altitudes and skimmed by clouds, we sensed our speed by how fast the clouds swept by. When we were high above the earth, we had little physical cues that made us feel we were flying at great speed. I got a real scare one time high over Nevada, and it vividly showed me what our speed looked like. About the only traffic we were told we might see above 70,000 feet, was an errant weather balloon. Although they were a rare sight, they were a hazard to aircraft. I never thought I would see one, but I did. First it appeared as a speck on my windscreen, then it instantly became a giant ball off to my right. There was no time to make an evasive turn or even think about turning. I could only watch in terror as it whisked passed us. I quickly looked in the mirror and saw the balloon flutter wildly from the passage of our shock wave. In an instant, it became a speck again. The entire episode took only a few seconds. By the time I informed Walt what I had just seen, it was long gone. That was the fastest I've ever seen anything move by me. I preferred to keep a sense of our speed by simply watching my distance measuring equipment (DME) click off a mile every two seconds.

Altitude could be deceiving too. Once as we made a run across Colorado, I noticed a range of snow-capped mountains that I thought extended from Pikes Peak in Colorado, to the border of New Mexico. I was used to flying military jets between 30,000 and 40,000 feet, and my eyes were calibrated to that scale. Upon close inspection, I realized I was looking at the segment of Rocky Mountains extending from Colorado to the Canadian border. I was gaining an entirely new perspective on the world below.

Once at altitude, the view from the cockpit was spectacular but normally went unappreciated because cockpit duties monopolized my attention. As my flight time in the jet increased, I occasionally took a few seconds to look outside. Even though these moments were brief, my memory of them was lasting.

A view from the top of the world. A stretch of the Rocky Mountains encompassing three states.

Though the RSO was responsible for navigation, I liked to keep up with our position throughout the flight. This was difficult to do by simply looking out the window. Computerized summaries of detailed information about our flight were provided, but I wanted a concise, easy to read depiction of my route of flight and its geography. Knowing precise latitude and longitude wasn't as important to me as knowing whether to turn right or left. Besides, I had Walt, an encyclopedia of information, to tell me details if I needed them.

After attempting different methods of cockpit housekeeping, I came up with a system I liked. I used an old high school geography book to trace an outline of the western United States and the state boundaries. Next I drew an approximation of our route, marking points where we would turn, refuel, and begin descents. This handmade map fit into a four by six-inch plastic protector that I put on my knee board. With my system, I could glance down, see where I was heading, and when the next turn would be.

Although this system was simple, it was valuable because it kept me oriented at high altitude and helped me make quick assessments of where to land if we had an emergency. When we started flying operational missions, I continued with my atlas-on-a-knee system. There was no room for a wrong turn then, and my knee drawings were a valuable tool for instant orientation.

Fortunately, my backseater operated a more sophisticated navigation system. The Astro-Inertial Navigation System (ANS) was a phenomenal system and we considered it our third crew member. Much like R2D2 in the Star Wars movies, it was placed into a special compartment behind the RSO's cockpit. It had its own cooling system that was kept within a few degrees of its prescribed temperature. The ANS could track up to 300 stars in broad daylight through its glass porthole atop the fuselage. It started functioning as soon as the aircraft left the hangar. It was a critical part of the mission; if it coughed, we turned around. Tapes describing our route of flight were fed into the ANS before takeoff, and once airborne, it interfaced with the autopilot system. The RSO spent a substantial time monitoring, checking, updating, and sometimes, just plain figuring out the ANS. It was a remarkable system and didn't fail often. I thought the ANS should have had its own little space suit.

Most people were under the impression the autopilot did all the flying, and the pilot sat there and monitored the gauges. The pilot did monitor the gauges all the time but he also controlled the airspeed and altitude. He regulated the Mach with the throttles throughout the flight and adjusted altitude by delicately moving a thumb-wheel control on the autopilot. The autopilot helped by controlling the ground track and told the jet when to turn along the route. Turns were made without the pilot making inputs on the stick.

We normally cruised in a very slight climb throughout the flight. As the jet became lighter due to fuel consumption, altitude was increased gently to optimize the range. As the air became thinner, less fuel was required to achieve the same thrust. Outside air temperature had the greatest influence on fuel consumption. Even though our forecasters were good, upper level temperatures were difficult to predict accurately. Warmer than standard temperatures at high altitude hurt performance by increasing fuel consumption. Colder than normal temperatures were a blessing and helped us 'make' gas en route. We could tell from cockpit indications, if the outside air temperature was different from what had been forecast. We used this information to seek the optimum altitude with the best temperature.

In addition to monitoring fuel quantity, maintaining the proper Mach, and adjusting altitude, I had several other cockpit chores: adjusting the center of gravity (CG), and closely monitoring engine temperatures and the positions of the spikes and the air bypass doors. The aircraft's center of gravity changed as fuel was burned. I continually monitored and adjusted it. To maintain an optimum CG, I transferred fuel forward or aft by operating fuel boost pumps. This not only provided a more stable airplane, but also reduced the drag.

By reducing drag, we saved fuel. Another way we reduced drag was by insuring the control surfaces were properly trimmed. Following the refueling, the rudders were sometimes out of alignment because they had been trimmed to offset flying with one burner lit. I checked rudder alignment by looking through a small periscope located at the top of the cockpit. I pushed the periscope into the slipstream and could see the rear of the aircraft. If I could see the rudders offset, I trimmed them flush with the vertical tail.

Engine temperatures were important to watch. Sometimes, they wandered out of the safe band, and I adjusted them back into the desired range with a lever in the cockpit. Spikes and air bypass door gauges warranted a million looks per flight, as mentioned earlier. If a spike were as little as an inch off, the inlet was operating inefficiently costing valuable fuel, and the likelihood of an unstart increased.

At the low altitudes, the jet required a strong arm to muscle the stick around. At high altitude, the pilot flew the airplane from the neck up. The pilot still controlled altitude and airspeed, but control inputs could not be abrupt. Flying faster than a speeding bullet made any control input noticeable. We could hand-fly the jet above

Mach 3 if the autopilot failed, as long as the stability augmentation systems were functioning. This required a concentrated effort and happened to us one day over Europe. I ended up hand-flying the airplane through the second half of the mission and I was able to hold it steady enough for the sensors to function effectively.

By the time I came to the program, the SR-71 had been fitted with a triple computer system that helped manage flight systems. This system was a valuable addition to the aircraft, but the computers did not fly the jet for me. Technicians told us the computers were highly reliable and the possibility of all three failing simultaneously was zero. I think the guys who issued that statement were brilliant engineers, but they never flew jets. Several months later, a crew was returning from Central America at high Mach and nearly had to eject. All three computers, amazingly enough, had failed simultaneously, and the aircraft was almost uncontrollable. It pitched up and the pilot was barely able to level it. It pitched up a second time, and he miraculously wrestled the jet to a semblance of controlled flight. He informed his RSO that if there were one more oscillation, he wouldn't be able to control it, and they would have to eject. At that moment, all three computers reset, and they were able to continue flying and landed safely. The RSO had a serious discussion with the computer specialists after that sortie.

THE SUIT

Flying in the space suit wasn't as uncomfortable as it looked. They were efficient in design and superbly maintained by PSD, so we rarely had any problems with them. A main valve controlled the amount of airflow to the suit. It was located on the front of the space suit and controlled the amount of air circulating through the space suit. Running airflow up to high was normally not done, because it inflated the suit slightly, taking up room in the cockpit. The suit torso contained flotation devices that increased the bulk of the space suit. After long hours of flight, I would increase the airflow to feel cool air gush across my body. Two separate rheostats controlled suit temperature, and heat to the face plate. The Suit Heat rheostat controlled the temperature of the air circulating in the suit. The Face Heat rheostat was used when the face plate on the helmet fogged up. It increased the flow of warm air across the face plate causing vapor to dissipate.

I had the added problem of wearing glasses. The stems were shortened, and the glasses were fixed to a small T-bar at the top of the helmet, held securely with Velcro. Occasionally the lenses fogged up, and I alleviated this problem by increasing airflow through the suit. Other than this, the glasses were never a problem. I never realized

Waiting for darkness, an SR-71 prepares for night
flight. These were always scary

how often I adjusted my glasses or scratched my face until I put on a space helmet. On the first few flights, I tried to scratch my face only to find my fingers interrupted by a face plate I had forgotten was there.

The helmet had an adjustable dark visor to protect from the bright sun at high altitude. Using the dark visor was not always helpful. Bright sunlight caused glare on the gauges and provided a large contrast to the shade in the cockpit. Pulling the dark visor down made reading instruments nearly impossible under these conditions. The solution was lowering the sunshades to block the sun and wearing the visor in the up position. The sunshades were similar to the sun visors found in automobiles. They could be moved in a variety of positions and even expanded to cover a greater area. As the jet proceeded through different phases of flight, the pilot continually repositioned the shades to block glare so he could clearly see important instruments. Refueling on a sunny day was one time where the dark visor was used.

The only serious problem I encountered with my space suit was when I lost suit heat in the middle of a sortie. The cockpit did not have vents to provide warm air like other airplanes. With the suit heat inoperative, the overall cold wasn't too bad on my body, because the space suit offered some protection. But my hands began to feel the numbing cold and I was starting to lose the feel of my fingers through the gloves. I remembered from training that the windows in the cockpit heated to about 550 degrees Fahrenheit when cruising at Mach 3. We were going faster than that so I knew the windows must be warm even on the inside. I placed my gloved hand against the window. In seconds, my hand was not just warm, it was hot. With care, I was able to complete the mission by intermittently warming my hands by gently placing them against the windows.

NIGHT

Part of our training included learning to fly the SR-71 at night. Night flying in any aircraft was challenging, but it was even more difficult in the Sled. The airplane's cockpit lighting had changed very little since it was first built, and the old-style system did not uniformly illuminate all the gauges. If the lights were turned up so the dimmest gauge could be easily read, the cockpit flooded with light that bounced off the inward canting of the side windows and the sharp-angled front windscreen. The windscreens became mirrors reflecting the cockpit scene back to me, and obstructed my ability to see out. By turning the lights down low, I reduced these distracting reflections and could more easily see important things like other aircraft, or the runway. I had to make a trade-off between being able to read all the instruments, or being able to see outside. During aerial refueling, I spent most of the time staring at the tanker's director lights and didn't need to study cockpit gauges, so the lights remained dimmed. Once we started the acceleration maneuver, I turned the cockpit lighting up. We weren't as concerned with seeing and avoiding other traffic at the altitudes we frequented. Above 50,000 feet, the sky was ours. My cockpit became a womb of brightly lit instruments climbing into the black sky. With no outside references, I sometimes felt as if we were in the simulator instead of the jet.

Whether the moon was full or in its last quarter, it dominated the sky. High above the haze and pollution of the earth's atmosphere, its light was so intense, I had to squint when I looked outside. I could see more of the moon's surface and its craters and textures than I had ever seen from the ground. Sometimes I had to use the sunshades to block the moonlight's glare from disrupting my view of the gauges.

I described earlier how fuel seeped through the minute seams outlining the panels composing the surface of the jet. Although little leakage occurred when the skin heated up and sealed the seams, some fuel remained on the surface. Through the periscope, I could see the moon's incandescent image shimmering in the residual fuel. The top of the aircraft glowed in the eerie light, like a wet street after a downpour. Although this was beautiful, I was more intrigued by the sights in a dark sky on a certain night when there was no moon at all.

It happened during the early hours of the morning, while Walt and I were over the Pacific, having passed the northwest coast of the United States. We were heading, in a round about way, back toward Beale. Our jet was running smoothly and we would soon be home resting our weary bodies after another training mission. With no moon above and no lights from the ocean below, the night was darker than usual. Out of habit, I peered outside through the glare of the cockpit lighting and noticed the faint glimmer of stars. To fully see the night sky, I would have to turn down important cockpit lights to reduce the glare on my windows. I was reluctant to turn my lighting too far down because I didn't want to be in an awkward position if something were to go wrong with the airplane.

Desire to see the stars overruled my caution and I began to turn the lights down one at a time, carefully leaving a few critical gauges well lit. My eyes adjusted to the lower level of light and I gradually saw more stars through the remaining reflections on the windows. On impulse, I flicked the remaining lights off, then quickly back on. An image flashed through my head of a teenager driving down a dark country road who flicks his headlights off for a second, is enveloped by darkness, then flicks them back on. I chuckled at the comparison. The jet reassured me as it purred rock solid, so I turned the remaining lights off. I was immediately startled; were those the lights of another aircraft out to my right? My disbelief soon turned to awe as I realized in the calm darkness, that what I saw was not the bright lights of any man-made vehicle, but the brilliant expanse of the Milky Way. Unlike the view from the ground, at 78,000 feet there were few spaces unlit in the sky. Shooting stars appeared and faded every few seconds. The spectacle was mesmerizing, but I knew I must bring my eyes back to the flight instruments. When I did, I discovered my entire cockpit bathed in starlight, bright enough to illuminate all the gauges. I needed no cockpit lighting and revelled in the ghostly sight of my space suit dimly lit in the starlight.

Feeling I was stealing precious moments from a jealous jet, I glanced once more outside. With all those clusters of light, it seemed as if there should be sounds. My experience told me sounds went with great displays of light. City lights coexist with the sounds of traffic, and rockets firing and exploding coincide with the display of fireworks. Even a planetarium has music and narration accompanying the sequence of stars. In contrast, this sight was a symphony of silence. I became very aware of the sound of my own breathing. For a brief moment I was more than an Air Force pilot on a training flight. Our incredible speed became insignificant as the jet seemed to stand still before the heavens. I was part of something larger and more profound. I felt a joy to be at this place, at this time, looking at these stars.

Walt's voice crackled over the intercom, jolting me back to the tasks at hand with a reminder of our upcoming descent. I turned the lights back up and left that peaceful yet powerful scene. As we started down, I didn't know that this was the last time I would experience this concert of stars. Although I flew on dark and moonless nights again, they were never routine enough to turn off the lights and cruise by starlight.

RECOVERY

We descended from high altitude between two to four times during one flight, usually to meet a tanker holding at 20,000 to 25,000 feet. The descent had to begin by the preplanned point in the flight or else we risked overrunning the tanker at the rendezvous point. Since the descent took a couple hundred miles to complete, correcting for a late start down was difficult. Most crews had zipped past the tanker

Returning from a training mission, the Sled comes down to mortal speeds and altitudes.

"We did Nebraska in 7½ minutes today. I think that's the best way to do Nebraska."

SLED PILOT

at one time or another, helpless at slowing the aircraft any quicker. After taking on fuel, we would climb back to altitude to continue our mission or cruise back to the base.

I pulled the throttles out of afterburner to military power as soon as we reached the planned descent point. Once the afterburners were disengaged, there was no choice; the jet was definitely coming down. A steep angle of descent was required to keep an adequate amount of air flowing through the engines. Bringing the jet down from altitude was not as hectic as taking it up, but it required every bit as much attention. The SR didn't slow down easily. No drag devices like flaps, spoilers, or air brakes existed, so it cut through the air like a sharp knife. A senior crew told us one technique (flying this airplane seemed like just one big collection of techniques) for slowing the plane down: fully open one air bypass door and spill engine air overboard. This caused drag and helped slow the aircraft down. I tried it and it worked. With the dumping of air from the bypass doors and the forward movements of the spikes as the airspeed slowed, the jet made noises that weren't heard any other time. I felt as if she hated coming down.

Once subsonic, the jet was again like a big fighter, with its inlet system operating much like that of other airplanes. Normally, training flights were planned to give the pilot extra fuel to practice some landing patterns. Pilots appreciated this because they knew they wouldn't get much landing practice during real missions. RSOs weren't too thrilled with numerous patterns though. There wasn't much for them to do except notice just how hot their space suits became at low altitude.

The jet was stable on final approach, but required the pilot to plan ahead. At close to 200 knots approach speed, there was not much opportunity to make last minute corrections. After cruising in clear skies at altitude for most of the flight, coming back to bad weather for landing could be a jolt to a fatigued body. In the landing pattern, the jet was surprisingly agile for its size, and when it was low on fuel, it responded rapidly to changes in power settings, even at low airspeed. We never pressed the fuel, which meant we never tried to squeeze in one more pattern if we had a little extra gas. The airplane guzzled gas at an alarming rate at low altitudes.

Our sim instructors warned us about the opening shock of the large drag chute on landing, and it was every bit as strong as advertised. The drag chute was nice to have, because it shortened our landing roll. It was especially handy when we were forced to land at an emergency airfield along our route. Not all airports built their runways as long as those in Strategic Air Command. After landing I looked through the periscope to determine if the chute were still inflated before jettisoning it. If the chute had deflated before I released it, the buckle connecting the chute to the airplane might hit the tail.

Passing by Mount Lassen, the rigors of the mission are over and the crew heads south for landing at Beale.

Once we taxied off the runway, the mobile car guided our path back to the hangar. It was only then I began to feel the drain of the past several hours. Popping off the gloves and loosening the helmet felt great. My body, which had been on adrenaline most of the past several hours, now began to feel stiff and fatigued. It was a good fatigue; exhaustion that was the result of meaningful effort.

Taxiing into the shutdown area, we were always greeted by a large number of maintenance people, technical representatives, mobile crew, PSD, and any visitors who were being escorted on the ramp. Normally following a flight, we were hungry and couldn't wait to get out of our space suits. No matter what our mission, we always felt relief, joy and satisfaction each time we returned. Each mission flown increased the bond of trust and respect between pilot and RSO. In the Blackbird, I experienced a greater sense of accomplishment at the end of a good flight, than in any other jet I had flown.

It was hard to sleep after a long mission, even though I was exhausted. It took a while for the adrenaline to subside. Often I would stay up late into the night feeling my inner ears pop and squeak from the effects of long hours of breathing one hundred percent oxygen.

As we progressed through our training flights, I began to feel more comfortable in the jet. Most of us would never be completely comfortable in the airplane because we didn't get to fly it more than one or two times a week. She would talk to me in flight, and the more I got to know her, the more she'd tell me. She had many secrets, and it seemed as if she enjoyed sharing them with me in her own time.

She was an armful in the landing pattern, but pilots rarely rushed to put her on the ground.

"... Some mornings I'd see more of the United States in three hours than most folks would see in a lifetime ...."

SLED RSO

Large drag chute was deployed on every landing, greatly reducing the landing distance.

Sled taxis in after flight. Open drag chute doors can be seen on top rear of jet.

An RSO starts to shed the suit after a long flight.

The traditional handshake after each flight. Many tight bonds of friendship formed from years of flying together.

CHAPTER IV

Going Operational

There came a time, finally, when training was completed and we were ready to fly our first operational sortie. The SR-71 flew operational sorties from Beale, Okinawa in the Pacific, and England. From these three locations, the SR could cover the globe. Normally the squadron had 10 to 15 mission-ready crews. This wasn't many pilots considering the scope of the mission. Squadron life after training meant spending most of a calendar year overseas. The crews accepted this hardship, and the frequency of leaving home for a month or two at a time was a burden for the families left behind. Crews couldn't talk about work and this increased their loved ones' anxiety. Sometimes, friends and family could figure out where we were flying by watching the evening news.

Okinawa was the first stop for a new crew. Okinawa was a good place to start because the sorties were less complex, and the weather was generally better than in Europe. When the SR-71 first came to the island early in the program, it did not go unnoticed by the locals. Intrigued by the ominous shape of the aircraft, Okinawans began calling it "Habu." The Habu was a poisonous black viper indigenous to the island, and residents felt the jet resembled the deadly snake. Squadron members adopted the nickname, and it stuck. A shoulder patch worn by SR-71 crew members simply read HABU. It had two stars at the top signifying the two men in the airplane. Crew members received their HABU patches only after they flew their first operational sortie.

When Walt and I returned from our first real mission in Okinawa, our mobile crew sadly informed us that the squadron supply of patches had run out, and we would have to receive ours later. As we tried to understand how this could happen, they reached into the leg pockets of our space suits and pulled out several HABU patches amidst much laughter. They told us how they had slipped them in our suits the day before, figuring we'd like to wear patches that had accompanied us on our first mission. It was a nice gesture.

After a full tour in Okinawa and a return to Beale, crews were prepared for sorties in the European theater. Crews flew simulator missions that depicted typical European routes. These routes were more complex and challenging because there were so many borders and associated restrictions to our flight path. In Europe we were forced to fly many more steep-banked turns at high Mach than in the Pacific. We also had to reduce our Mach to help increase our turn rate, and this was uncomfortable in high threat areas. These simulators were excellent preparation for this upcoming tour.

Once training was completed, the Jet took on a new look to the crew. Missions had a deadly serious purpose now.

My main objective during a mission was to keep the jet on the preplanned route, sometimes called the black line. If we got off the black line, or if the jet malfunctioned, we came home. If the jet were seriously broken, we landed at one of the emergency airfields along the route. Either way, we never took the risk of having even one piece of the jet touch hostile soil.

Although getting the images gathered by the sensors was important, we avoided unnecessary risks. The unspoken word was that no part of this aircraft would ever fall into the other side's hands. As a pilot, I felt as if my life were in danger on every mission. Often the regime in which we flew harbored more potential danger than the other side's offensive abilities. I feared no one while flying the SR-71 in pursuit of its mission. My confidence was born out of increased experience in the jet.

Many times we never saw the images we brought back. Our job was only to collect them; others interpreted them. Many people were interested in receiving the product the jet brought back. These people included senior ranking members of the Department of Defense, the Defense Intelligence Agency, the Central Intelligence Agency, and even the President of the United Sates. Most of the time we never knew who these people were. If we did our job properly, everyone else was satisfied. Many days I felt as if I were sitting at the tip of the sword of a system that was larger in scope than I could imagine. There were many important people who took what we did seriously, but nobody took this work more seriously than the guy with his hand on the stick.

On rare occasions, the photo interpreters showed us the product of our labor. This gave us a better perspective of the process involved in interpreting hundreds of feet of film, and an appreciation for the resolving power of cameras shooting through heat soaked windows. On one occasion after a mission in the Caribbean, the photo folks showed us some pictures they thought we would find interesting. They depicted parts of a gunnery range used by Cuban fighter jets to sharpen their strafing skills. On close inspection, the pictures revealed the targets were large silhouettes of SR-71s painted on cloth. We considered this a compliment of sorts. The next time over that route, I pushed the Mach up slightly to insure they would hear the boom.

Although the Sled was ahead of its time with stealth-like design, it was not invisible. At high Mach, extreme temperatures covered the aircraft like a warm glove. This heat source did not go unnoticed by countries that preferred not to have their pictures taken. The Sled also left a bold signature written across its flight path: a healthy sonic boom. Certain foreign governments didn't like this sound over their heads, but I wasn't too enamored with some of their practices and was always pleased to bring it to them.

The HABU patch was a prized collector's item. It was also hard-earned by each crew member and seldom relinquished to souvenir hunters.

Emblem outside the SR-71 squadron building in England.

The run-up area in Okinawa. Sunny days like this were always welcome.

At any one time, I knew I was one of a dozen or so pilots in the world flying the Blackbird. After flying it for a while, I was also aware of the many people behind the scenes who made it possible for me to do my job. Launching one Sled on one sortie involved hundreds of people, each performing their own special task that could ultimately affect the outcome of the mission. The number of people involved wasn't much smaller on training missions either. This concentration of effort for one flight impressed me and instilled in me a sense of purpose and pride I had rarely experienced in other endeavors.

Long before the crew ever arrived for their weather brief, maintenance people had been preparing the jet for flight. Lights aglow in the hangar at midnight usually meant the jet would launch at 9 or 10 o'clock the next morning. The SR required more than the average jet to prepare for flight. Viscous lubricants that sustained high temperatures in flight needed to be preheated. The Tetraethyl Borane, used for starting the engines and igniting the afterburner, was loaded into the engine. This was a hazardous procedure because it could ignite on contact with oxygen. The tires and two tanks in the forward nose were filled with nitrogen. Nitrogen stored in the forward nose was used to pressurize the fuel tanks; it reduced the risk of fuel vapors igniting from heat build up. This servicing of nitrogen gave the jet a mystical presence as white clouds of vapor streamed from its nose. Numerous diagnostic checks were run on the computers and the navigational systems. The SR-71 could be fitted with different noses, each providing a different reconnaissance capability. The proper nose was loaded onto the aircraft depending on what type of mission was being flown.

While maintenance was preparing the jet, mission planners were drawing the routes, making the maps, and producing computer printouts for the crew. Because of the special sensor-related duties the RSO performed, the information packet he received was always a bit thicker than the pilot's. One of the planners would normally meet with the crew at the preflight meal and brief them on any special details.

Across the airfield, the men and women who flew the KC-135Q tankers were preparing for their mission. They were given orbit points where the rendezvous would occur, and the time they could expect to see the Blackbird arrive behind them. Sometimes three or four tankers would take part in one mission. The tankers launched many hours before the SR. They orbited, off-loaded the fuel, then returned, usually arriving home long after the Sled had landed. Tanker crews received little of the attention and praise others shared, but they were proud of their part in the SR-71's

The guys that kept us flying.

Civilian crew chief monitors engine start and communicates to pilot on headset.

Long before the crew arrived, maintenance was doing its job. Here the large intakes are being inspected. The sharpness of the spike warranted tip covers.

missions. They knew they were essential. A boom operator once told me that the Sled was a relatively easy aircraft to refuel from his end. He added that no matter how many times he refueled it, the Blackbird was an imposing sight. While searching the empty sky behind the tanker, he would suddenly see this black shark looming out of the void. Every Sled pilot around knew what it felt like to be low on gas, far, far from home. During those times, the sight of one KC-135 was nothing less than beautiful.

In addition to all the Air Force people supporting the aircraft, a host of civilian specialists worked on the SR-71. Companies who had systems on the SR assigned technical representatives, or tech reps, to work at Beale and the overseas detachments. Some of these systems were basic aircraft components like Goodyear tires. Other systems, produced by Honeywell or Singer, were more complex and sometimes classified. The crews got to know these folks well and learned a great deal from them about the magic in the airplane. Many of the tech reps worked on the program for many years and possessed valuable corporate knowledge the military lost to transfers and retirements.

At our detachment in England, regular Air Force maintenance specialists were replaced by civilian Lockheed employees. Ranging in age from late twenties to early sixties, this group of people handled the launch and maintenance of the jet daily. They dressed casually for work and could easily pass for a group of visitors that came to watch the jet takeoff. On our first tour to England, I had a small problem in flight with an engine and wanted to talk with an engine man after landing. I was told I could talk with the chief who was somewhere around the back end of the airplane. I walked around the jet and the only person I could locate was a short, elderly man wearing grease and oil stained coveralls and wire frame glasses. I studied this slightly balding man wiping his hands in a fuel stained cloth. He had the face of a man who had seen and done much. He politely inquired if he could be of some assistance to me. He had a light in his eyes and a warmth to his smile that let me know I had found the chief. His name was "Doc," and that's all we ever knew him by. He had more years working on these engines than I had years of flying. He had been on the project back in "the old days" and knew more about how to fix and maintain the engines than anyone else around. Here was a man who truly loved his work. Over the years I deployed to England, I got to know Doc well. After many flights, I relished in the opportunity to confer with the master on matters of thrust immediately after climbing out of the jet. Doc was typical of the type of dedicated expert we were privileged to work with. Whenever I taxied the black beast out of the hangar on a rainy day, I felt the support,

The chief listens and watches as the Sled readies for takeoff. No one did it better.

Every landing required a chute, and every chute required a pick-up.

pride, and dedication of those people right there with me. They never got to fly the airplane, but I know that many of them loved her as much as I did.

Flying operational missions out of Beale usually meant keeping strange hours. My neighbors wondered about me when I left for the base at two o'clock in the morning. The people in the Marysville-Yuba City area, though, seemed to take pride in knowing that the world's fastest jet resided at 'their' Air Force base. They appreciated knowing I couldn't tell them details of where I was flying or what I was doing. They enjoyed the intrigue. On several occasions I stopped at the local 7-11 for an orange juice on my way to work, sometimes after midnight. The same man worked the graveyard shift, and he'd look up and smile. I'd say 'Good morning' as I walked to the refrigerated case. In the beginning, he was eager to tell me that he had a good idea what I was doing, and he wished me good luck. Above all, he did not want me to reveal anything to him. I never could say much, because he did most of the talking. Sometimes, his assessment of my mission routing was surprisingly accurate. Later on, I'd come in and he'd say, "So, just going to work?" On these mornings we had an unspoken camaraderie; the two of us shared a few moments of the early morning hours. It gave him pleasure to insist I not pay for the juice.

WEATHER

Our training at Beale prepared us for what we would be doing overseas, with one exception: weather. The central valley of northern California did not approximate the weather patterns of either Okinawa or England. Beale spoiled us with clear days and rare storm systems. Okinawa weather also could be wonderful at times, but it was unpredictable. Another factor complicated the weather equation; a small island in the Pacific didn't leave a pilot with many options for diverting someplace else if the weather got bad. England was more predictable; the weather was lousy all the time. After a few weeks in sunny California, I would find myself sitting in English fog on an icy runway, preparing to launch into murky weather seldom seen at Beale.

Some days while taxiing out of the hangar in England, I had a tough time seeing the mobile car through the fog. Experienced crews were tested time and time again, as they launched on missions in poor weather conditions. Weather rarely stopped our missions.

Flying high up in the stratosphere and managing complex systems produced enough tension for most, but sometimes the first few minutes of the flight were filled with the most excruciating tension of the day. I sat through a weather briefing one day in Okinawa that described a violent storm system. I was amazed at the fury nature could generate,

Beale tanker displays nose art reflecting the local area. The camouflage paint scheme was not popular with Sled pilots because the darker airplane was harder to see in bad weather.

A pair of KC-135Qs taxi out well before the SR-71 would take off.

Pilot prepares for takeoff. In a couple hours he'll be over hostile territory.
First, he must get through the hostile weather.

and that our mission was important enough to still launch despite the extreme weather. The briefer listed the typhoon warnings but added our takeoff time would permit a safe launch. I remember thinking we should put this man through pilot training so he could get a new perspective on the word safe concerning flying in weather.

As Walt and I climbed into the jet, we noticed across the field flying had been cancelled for the day, and crew chiefs were tying down the F-15s. As I settled into the plane among an array of connections, I felt comfortable and secure in the cockpit and space suit, despite the threatening outside elements. A PSD specialist wiped raindrops from the faceplate of my space helmet. After engine start, I engaged nose wheel steering by pushing a small button on the stick, and taxied into the rain. Watching the gray walls of clouds at the end of the runway planted a seed of anxiety in my cozy environment. As I turned the jet into the run-up area, I felt a sinking feeling of being slightly out of control. Even with brakes applied, the jet was sliding forward on the slippery film of rain soaked coral dust on the taxiway. Sitting in front of 50 tons of titanium and fuel that was sliding toward the mobile car was not a good way to start the day.

Trailing a spray of mist from a wet runway, the Sled lifted off and smoothly pulled skyward. As I reached for the landing gear handle, the jet was engulfed in a tomb of swirling rain. Dark gray clouds seemed to fill the cockpit. The plane accelerated undaunted by the elements, and I concentrated on the instruments before me.

Without outside visual references, my perception of the climb began to lag what the jet was actually doing. The acceleration in full burner, the high angle of climb, and the gentle turn onto the departure routing, took place while I was enveloped in the mass of gray clouds. My 'seat-of-the-pants' feel of the airplane's bank angle and pitch attitude disagreed with what the instruments were saying. My eyes read the instruments that said one thing, but my body told me something different. This confusion between visual information and the body's sensation is called spatial disorientation. It can undermine even the most experienced pilot and is difficult to shake once induced. The best cure is to find some clear sky, see the horizon, and get orientated.

As we climbed higher, the sky grew darker and heavy turbulence buffeted the jet. In these conditions, the Sled's fuselage flexed slightly, causing the front end of the plane to bend more than the rear section. From the cockpit, I felt a little like I was being bounced on the end of a titanium diving board. Controlling the aircraft was not made any easier and Walt informed me we were slightly off course.

I was late in coming out of afterburner. Sweat pooled inside my gloves and my grasp tightened on the stick and throttles. I felt warm inside the space suit, and noticed fog forming on my faceplate. Because I felt we were flying near up-side-down, the simple

Climbing out on a foggy day in England.

"Missions were intense from start to finish. It was the ultimate in job satisfaction."

SLED PILOT

task of reaching for the Face Heat knob was a struggle. The conflict waging between my senses was eased by Walt reassuring me we were level. Random lightening illuminated the angry clouds around me like flash bulbs popping off on a camera. Rain pelted the outside of the cockpit as if we were passing through a car wash. Surely I should be able to hear the racket caused by the punishing downpour, but the space helmet and the four inch thick glass in the cockpit muffled the outside sounds. Only the strained rhythm of my own breathing accompanied my struggle to right my tilted senses. I tried to engage the autopilot to reduce my workload, but the turbulent conditions caused it to kick off after each attempt. I watched the wrath of nature unfold just inches from where I sat and felt a great sense of comfort in the solid construction around me.

It seemed like an eternity before the jet broke free from the clouds and soared into a clear piece of sky. There had been no sense of motion while we were in the gray mass below us, but now I instantly became aware of our speed as chunks of clouds sped by at 350 knots. As a spinning top decelerates, it wavers and finally falls on its side. If this were recorded on film and then run backwards, the top would go from teetering to instant stability as it reached the higher rate of revolutions. My brain accelerated in the same way as we bolted from the clouds, and it immediately aligned itself with our true flight orientation.

Breaking out on top of the weather was one of the untold joys of an aviator. In one short moment, relief and happiness replaced tension and exertion as the act of flying changed from a hellish nightmare to a beautiful scene of white cloud tops and blue sky. I had been airborne a total of eight minutes and was exhausted. In another ten minutes I would be trying to hook up with the tanker in the clouds I saw forming in the refueling track. I said a couple of "Hail Kelly Johnsons" and realized I could trust the Sled more than the weatherman.

I always had a healthy respect for the forces of weather; flying the SR-71 only reaffirmed this respect. I often heard that some thunderstorms could build to 60,000 feet and the SR-71 made me a believer. Walt and I watched with amazement as we finally broke out into the clear at 72,000 feet one afternoon over the South China Sea.

We were cautious about penetrating bad weather, but we never worried much about flying in icing conditions. The jet's surfaces heated up from friction between the skin and the high speed air passing over it. Even though there was no anti-ice system on the aircraft, no ice stuck to the airplane due to the normal buildup of heat. The SR had no weather radar and sometimes we ended up penetrating some nasty weather.

A solitary figure emerges from the intense weather over the North Sea. Rain soaked and streaming JP-7, the Sled performed its mission while others dared not fly.

After hours in clear blue sky, coming back to a landing in poor weather was always a challenge.

Glad to be on the ground; the last ten minutes of flight were the most draining in weather like this.

Ingestion of ice chunks into the engine was our main concern. Not only could this damage the engine, it frequently could cause a flameout. Despite this hazard, the Sled just slammed right through icing conditions. It was a solid airplane, and when it was subsonic it exhibited a brute strength seldom found on today's high-tech jets. One day a KC-135Q returned to Beale and the post-flight inspection revealed a light on the belly of the aircraft was missing. Fearing an SR-71 engine may have ingested the light during the refueling, the Blackbird was recalled from its mission. Sure enough, after landing, the crew chiefs found evidence of the tanker's lower rotating beacon in the Sled's engine. The SR had chewed it up, spit it out, and never lost a beat. The crew had neither seen nor felt anything unusual. The aircraft was one tough machine.

EN ROUTE

Long missions meant hunger and thirst crept into the cockpit with us. The good folks at PSD learned what tube food and drinks the crews preferred and had them ready when they suited up. I normally carried a small water bottle and Walt took water and a couple tubes of butterscotch pudding. There wasn't much time to relax during a mission, but I would usually find a minute to drink from my water bottle during the descent to meet the tanker. Walt liked taking a snack break while I was completing the refueling. As I was fighting to take on the last few gallons of fuel, Walt would tell me about the quality of the butterscotch pudding that day.

I liked Walt's sense of humor in flight. In this line of work humor helped diffuse any tension. Enclosed in a cocoon of titanium and steel for hours at a time, we had to trust each other. A part of this included the man in back having faith that the guy in front would handle problems and fly the airplane skillfully. The RSO did not have any means to control the airplane if the pilot were incapacitated. If something happened to me, there was no option for Walt except to eject from the airplane.

One day, a simple problem made me realize the tenuous position Walt had, sitting in back with no stick. We were proceeding on a straight section of our route over Europe. This particular route had many turns, and the Mach had to be maintained precisely to prevent overshooting them. I decided to indulge in a quick drink from my water bottle before an upcoming turn. I put the long plastic straw to my helmet, located the opening and pushed, but nothing happened. Mildly frustrated, I pushed harder without success. I glanced in the mirror and found the straw in the right spot, so with one final shove, I pushed for the last time. The straw instantly slipped into my

In the calm dawn of morning, a pilot contemplates the mission ahead.

helmet, overshooting my mouth and poking my eye slightly. My eye began to tear profusely and at the same moment, Walt commanded a reduction in Mach to keep the turn radius under control. I forgot the water bottle and, seeing out of only one eye, concentrated on maintaining precise speed through the turn. My eye continued to tear as the airplane completed the turn remaining on course and on speed.

As I contemplated the possibility of finishing the mission and landing with one eye, I caught a glimpse of myself in the mirror. I saw a space helmet with a water bottle dangling out the lower section. I laughed out loud. Considering the seriousness of the business at hand, it was a ludicrous sight. Walt expressed his ignorance of what could be so funny at this particular moment. He added that he didn't want to know. I flew on one eye for a few hundred miles, then dried it out by using the Face Heat Switch.

From then on, I was careful when I performed even the simplest tasks. Later, when I achieved advanced proficiency with the water bottle, I found the straw was an excellent device for scratching my face slowly, very slowly. I never did tell Walt what happened that day over Europe. His confidence in me would probably not increase if he learned I had flown him through the stratosphere with a water bottle in my eye.

Checklists for both crew members were full of more information than anyone could possibly digest. In addition to these storehouses of knowledge, the guy in back carried additional manuals he could refer to when there was a problem. One morning over the South China Sea, a sensor light blinked in my cockpit, telling me the automated flight control system was malfunctioning. I attempted to reset the circuit to no avail, so Walt dove head first into the schematic diagrams stored in his manuals in the back cockpit. The more we tried to correct the problem, the more it defied us. Soon it threatened to bring our mission to an early end. We were approaching a point where we either had the system on line and could continue, or we didn't have the system and would have to return. I hated turning back on any mission. Out of frustration, I used a technique that worked once in a T-28. I slammed my hand against the sensor switch and cursed loudly in its direction. The channel reset, the light went out, and the jet performed flawlessly the rest of the day. So much for advanced engineering.

Most of the time the SR-71 was honest and rock solid, but when she got cranky at Mach 3, Walt and I had a bad day. Everyone else down the chain also had a bad day. Maintenance workers, tanker drivers, surveillance people, and rescue people, all had their days planned around our mission. All were affected when a sortie didn't go as planned. If we had an aircraft malfunction, our first responsibility was to get the jet down safely. In many cases the malfunction put us on the edge of safety.

High rolling across the Pacific. I got a real sense of just how much water there is out there. Okinawa never looked so small.

"I went through the entire training program without one unstart. Over North Vietnam, during the war, we got SAM missile warnings and the next thing I knew the aircraft was rocked violently. Of course I thought we were hit by an SA-2. Turned out to be our first unstart. What a time to have it . . . ."

SLED COMMANDER

One night near the Korean coast, the airplane was humming along beautifully. As we began a turn to the South, I momentarily took note of a fleet of well-lit fishing boats below me. My helmet striking against the side of the cockpit jolted me from the calm. The number one engine spike had lost hydraulic power and slammed forward, causing a violent unstart. Being in the turn only made the unstart worse. The engine continued in a series of unstarts as I wrestled to keep the jet under control and maintain our planned ground track. The increased yaw from the unstarts forced us slightly wide of the programmed turn. I'll always have a picture in my mind of that moment. In a dark sky, with both hands on the stick and the jet shaking violently, I tried to follow the calm instructions of my backseater, and avoid penetrating a sensitive area. Our sim training must have paid off as we luckily made it through one scary night. We limped home at subsonic speeds.

Even though the plane could be unpredictable, it seemed to perform its best on vital missions. The mission we flew over Libya was important; we had both airplanes in England up in the air that day. Our profile was stringent because of the hostile threat expected. Libya was not too happy about a recent visit by American F-111 fighter-bombers. We had just cleared the coast of England, and were flying at normal altitudes in search of our first tanker. I spotted traffic head-on and slightly below us. It was the F-111s returning from a long night's work. One less jet and crew flew in their formation. It was a silent moment. As the formation of fighter-bombers passed us, the lead aircraft rocked its wings, and I rocked ours in return.

All the way from England to Portugal our airplane gave us problems. It coughed and chugged, and let us know in many small ways it was going to be a pig that day. The doors and spikes rattled. It didn't make its time to climb and it burned more fuel that it was supposed to. The outside air temperatures were probably warmer than forecasted, and the jet was just not feeling good or accelerating as it should. Near Portugal we hit the tankers, then scooted across the Mediterranean area. The North African coast impressed me with its size. I was used to skipping across territories in a rapid fashion, but this leg was taking forever, even at high Mach. Checkpoint after checkpoint passed with disappointing aircraft performance. Walt pointed out that we weren't where we needed to be with our fuel remaining. Beginning the climb to our last checkpoint before the hot zone, I knew Walt wasn't confident about the airplane's ability to get up to our programmed speed in time to make our pass.

High above the Arctic Circle.

I knew this was an important mission; I wanted the jet to make it. I began moving the doors carefully, adjusting switches slowly, and talking to the airplane in a way known only to Gypsies, witch doctors, and single-seat fighter pilots, hoping things would improve. The airplane responded. It started to sound and feel different. All vibrations ceased, the doors quieted and the spikes became rigid. As we reached our last checkpoint, we were where we needed to be in speed and altitude. I said to Walt, "Hang in there. This jet is beginning to feel right." The airplane wasn't seriously broken, yet all of a sudden it was flying differently. As we crossed the target area, it was smooth as silk; not one vibration, not one unstart. As soon as we departed the hot zone, a few annunciators lit up in Walt's cockpit showing two missiles had been fired at us. We turned north, and our speed, altitude, and turn defeated the threat. Once we headed towards home, the airplane again began to perform poorly. It was as if it knew. After landing, we wrote up numerous malfunctions for maintenance. The airplane amazed me with ten minutes of smooth flying over Libya. After flying a number of sorties in the airplane, most pilots couldn't help thinking the airplane had a heart and spirit of its own.

MIG RUNNER

With an array of sensors in the rear seat, the RSO monitored many incoming signals during the flight. We were always alerted to signals indicating a hostile threat, either from a surface-to-air missile, or a fighter aircraft. Although we felt confident about the SR-71, we never took lightly any signals indicating a threat. The other side's threats were not a surprise to us, but they caused a face-off. They knew we were there, and we knew they were looking at us. We knew they would activate certain air defense systems, and they knew that it wasn't going to stop us from coming. Most of the time, it simply was not politically expedient for the other side to attempt to shoot us down, especially if they felt there were little chance of success. Although this was normally the case, we carried the memory of the 1981 incident with us all the time. In that year the North Koreans claimed violation of their airspace and fired a surface-to-air missile at an SR-71. It missed, but the crew witnessed the detonation of the missile from where they sat in the cockpit. We knew to expect the unexpected.

In areas we visited frequently, we came to expect distinct reactions. If we flew near air bases equipped with the latest Soviet MIG fighters, we expected to see the MIGs run intercepts on us. From all I had read, I knew this was common. No matter how good they were, they would have difficulty putting an air-to-air missile on a target moving faster than Mach 3. Normally we could only tell electronically that an

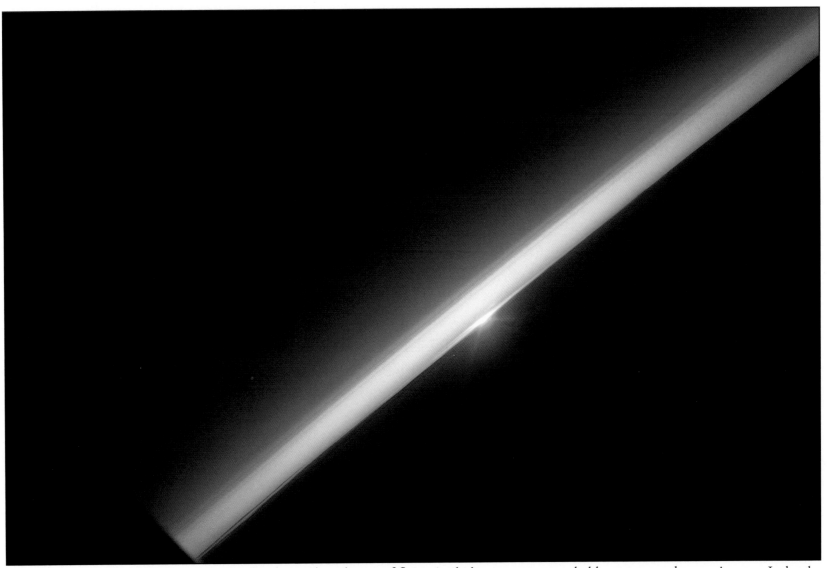

Ferrying the Jet from Beale AFB to England, my three hours of flying in darkness were rewarded by a spectacular sunrise over Iceland.

intercept attempt was in progress. I would scan a blank sky for signs of the interceptor but rarely saw them. At our speed and altitude, picking out a single jet far below me was difficult. On two different occasions though, I saw the brilliant white contrails of hostile fighters. I knew they would probably love to be the first to claim an SR-71 kill. They scrambled, hoping something would go wrong with my aircraft. We would be easy prey if we had to slow down and descend. With this thought in mind, I took pleasure in looking down at the rising contrails. By nudging the throttles forward I destroyed the straining fighters' opportunity for a successful intercept angle. In moments, the MIGs fell from view, wallowing in the thin air of upper altitudes. I couldn't help smiling as Walt's scope went blank and we darted toward home. I felt gratitude and pride in what Americans could build when given the chance. We had just mocked the finest modern-day MIGs in the world, with a jet nearly three times their age. John Wayne would have loved this airplane.

THE RETURN

Going to Okinawa on our first deployment was personally significant for me. Twelve years earlier, I arrived in Okinawa on a medical transport. I was transported to the intensive care unit at the Navy hospital located a few miles from the Air Force base. As one of the last casualties of the Vietnam campaign, I spent two months at the hospital before my condition improved enough so that I could endure the long flight back to the States. From my bed on the burn ward, I could see the East China Sea, a rocky beach, and a green soccer field. Many afternoons the turf filled with kids shouting and chasing a black and white ball from goal to goal. During that long two months, looking outside my window and seeing the rest of the world functioning normally took my mind off the pain.

I felt differently when I returned to that island, now flying the SR-71. I no longer saw the island through a small window from a hospital bed. I now saw it as a normal duty location and place where I could bike and swim in my free time. I was grateful for all that had transpired in the intervening years that had brought me back in this way. I found the green field again. Different kids played soccer with the same joy and normalcy. I watched and I wept. Though few noticed, every time I took off from the Air Force base, I banked sharply during the departure turn, taking my flight path towards the Naval base. I knew I covered a certain green field with a blanket of powerful sound.

Returning to Southeast Asia. The photo interpreters loved weather like this.

Most of our sorties from Okinawa took us north. On one occasion, we were tasked for a mission that took us south. It held more personal meaning for me than all the others I flew in the airplane. We reported for our pre-mission study the day before, and were handed maps showing an itinerary we had never seen before. We would fly across areas of Southeast Asia. This part of the world held many memories and stirred deep emotions in every man who had flown in the war. As we looked over the route, Walt and I exchanged stories of past days.

I was surprised to see our flight would take us over the area where my plane had gone down twelve years before. The last time I had seen this part of the world, I was being carried out on a stretcher. In the hospital they told me small arms fire had hit my airplane's engine. I remembered how little it mattered to me at the time because of my condition. I never imagined I would fly over this particular geography again. As Walt and I completed our mission preparation, I was glad we were returning to this land in this way.

The mission weather briefing the next day informed us the weather would be clear throughout the target areas. The weather briefer, the PSD folks, and the maintenance people were all a little more "up". Everyone seemed to know this was an unusual mission. As I walked from the van to the jet, a young maintenance airman approached me. He had seen my business card which said "This boom's for you," and asked if I would drag an extra loud boom today in honor of his father who was still listed as Missing In Action from the Vietnam War. His voice cracked with emotion, and I assured him we would be pleased to honor his father in this way.

After taking off and turning the airplane extra tight at the end of the runway, we proceeded south. Nearing the target area, we found the weather was as good as predicted. With the exceptional visibility, I could look down and see the long stretches of concrete composing airfields constructed by U.S. forces long ago. Where once rows of American fighters sat poised for battle, I now saw MIGs parked on the ramp. Looking at it now from the larger perspective provided by my cockpit, it made me sad. Could this land mass have been worth all those sorties, all those years, all those lives?

The Sled was performing flawlessly. We were crossing terrain I had once known intimately. Places I had seen at 200 miles per hour I now passed over at ten times that speed. Memories of long ago returned to my mind like old friends. Prominent landmarks echoed with voices from an era that now seemed so distant, but still familiar.

Earlier, Walt and I had identified the segment of our route which would take us over the area where my life had almost ended. As we approached it, Walt, always the friend, took a moment from his duties to alert me to look outside. I don't recall him ever reminding me to look outside and I appreciated his gesture. I had already been looking out for some time. I felt my hand moving the throttles forward.

As the Sled raced forward, my mind filled with flashbacks of all that followed the last time I had passed this nameless spot on the map. In only seconds, many images flashed in my mind: the horror of the moment when I knew my plane was going into the jungle; the quiet of the jungle floor, as I lay there listening to the sickening sound of my airplane burning; the eternity of those first two months in intensive care, when the numbness had worn off and I wanted to die; the long hours of painful physical therapy administered by people smart enough to ignore my protests; the doctors telling me I would never fly again; the surgical fusing of small bones in the hand that left steel pins temporarily protruding through tender fingers; my release from the hospital; the joy I felt on my first flights. Memory of it all rushed back to me as we passed over that fateful spot.

There were no steel pins now, just the firm grip of a gloved hand on metal throttles. The only surgery being performed was in the precision of our ground track as we dragged our sonic boom across a faceless jungle. I brought no weapons this day, but hoped the people below would hear the sound of freedom. I wanted the boom to shout with defiance "I'm back!" I felt proud to return in the black jet, undefeated. I also felt anger about the loss of so many who would never return.

As we approached a sensitive border, Walt politely reminded me that our Mach was too high, and I needed to reduce it. With a trace of reluctance, I complied. As we sped away from that scarred land, I took one last look at a place I would never forget. There was no pain at 78,000 feet.

After Walt and I climbed out of the jet that day, we shook hands as people do who have shared a special experience. As I was about to step into the van, I noticed the young airman, and gave him a "thumbs up." He returned the signal with a passion I could understand.

A barren, hostile land, with no signs of life except for the signals my RSO receives.

EAST

With all that was going on in the cockpit, it was a wonder I ever had a chance to look outside. Besides being so busy, the sunshades used to block the harsh glare of the sun, also obstructed the view. When I did find a moment to look outside, I would often see what I called 'virgin' geography. Virgin geography was land over which I would normally never fly, had I not been flying the Blackbird. Some days it was so clear I could see forever. One time while flying close to a particularly hostile nation, I couldn't help noticing the scenic panorama below me. Summer afternoon thunderstorms embraced a rugged mountain range. My eyes followed the storm pattern across the land and I realized the same line of building clouds extended across the border into the other side's territory. More striking still, the mountains that rose gracefully in each land were all part of the same range. The earth knew no lines of demarcation; it didn't adhere to the borders drawn on our maps. The range of mountains and the line of thunderstorms were apolitical. The clouds were no less white, and the sun shone just as brightly, on the other side. I thought for a moment how people could be so separated by ideas, words and boundaries, yet from where I sat, the earth was all part of one integrated pattern of random harmony. It was sad that those who ruled across the unseen border in that beautiful scene, had brought tyranny to an entire nation of people. Sadder still was the thought that someone down there heard my aircraft and thought I was the enemy. Walt alerted me we were being tracked by hostile radar and I pushed up the Mach. For a moment I had seen the world with great clarity.

WEST

Because of the higher latitude of England, winter days were very short. As Walt and I took off from England at mid-morning one cold January day, I had no idea that I was about to witness sights that would become the most memorable scenes in my twenty years of flying.

Our route took us far north. During our first aerial refueling, two Norwegian F-16 fighters joined on our wing as we slowed to rendezvous with our tanker. They provided a friendly escort and seemed to enjoy having our aircraft become part of their

A self portrait, helmet visor reflects the view from the top of the world. Reflection shows hand on stick, checklist on knee, and harsh contrast of sunlight and shadow on instrument panel. Camera is seen "baking" on dash.

formation. This kind of meeting was unplanned and rarely occurred. I knew they couldn't stay long, as our course was taking them further away from their base. Soon they would have their own low fuel status to contend with. Nevertheless, like teenagers in hot rods, these young Allied pilots seemed interested in a bit of a drag race. As I came off the tanker and cleared to the right, the fighters positioned themselves abeam me, waved, and lit their afterburners. I gave them a head start. The F-16 is a nice little jet and we enjoyed their visit. We left them in the dust.

We proceeded further north and crossed the Arctic Circle. The barren cold land below made me appreciate the warmth of my space suit, and wonder about the poor devils manning the facilities we had come to see. Comments from the back seat assured me that someone was down there. Walt had warnings on his scope. I checked the periscope and noticed we were leaving large contrails across the sky, formed from our exhaust hitting the cold air. Vapor in the exhaust instantly froze into ice crystals making dual white lines across the sky. When we had a hostile threat below, we preferred not to pull contrails because they pinpointed our location. The SR-71 didn't leave contrails often, so we rarely concerned ourselves about inadvertently leaving this advertisement. When we did leave contrails though, we continued our flight, making no deviations.

I noticed the large plumes emanating from the engines, and saw the sun setting on the horizon far to the South. The sunset seemed out of place, since we had left in the morning and had only been airborne for a couple of hours. I saw firsthand, how the tilt of the earth in winter months caused early sunsets at northern latitudes. I didn't think much more about this until we started a large right turn back toward the land masses to the South. As the nose of the jet tracked through the turn and we started heading eastward, I saw the most unusual sight. Out the right window I saw the light remaining from a setting sun. A pale blue sky was painted with red ribbons of light pointing to where the sun had just been. As I looked out the left window to the North, I saw a night sky, complete with stars. I had seen the sky at dusk many times while mountain climbing, and was familiar with the contrast of a departing sun and approaching darkness from higher altitudes. I had never seen a sunset this far North, and this high up. I had to look left and right several times to confirm what I was seeing. From our altitude, it was truly daytime on my right and nighttime on my left. As we continued through the right turn to the West, I was surprised to see our old contrails still painted across the sky. The two track pattern from our dual exhaust sketched our

Dusk at high altitude of northern latitudes. Daylight on my left, and moonrise and night to my right.

path through the evening sky. The contrails were no longer white, but now exhibited a golden reddish color. Each ice crystal sharply reflected the fiery hues of the setting sun. I viewed the subtle colors of the sky with the signature of the Sled arcing across it in lines of red, and realized I could never photograph this scene. The large contrast of light and dark would make the scene impossible to capture adequately on film. Nevertheless it held my attention until our final turn to the South.

We sped home in search of our third refueling, and the sun appeared to rise again as we travelled south. The sky returned to its normal color of deep blue. We left a strange and mysteriously beautiful area behind and returned to a land where the sun was where it should be. After landing we had much to debrief about mission-related material. Later, I mentioned the sight I had witnessed to Walt, and found he had been unable to see it because he was so busy at the time. As I walked back to my quarters, I watched the sun set for the second time that day. It had been a memorable flight. I'll always recall that picture of being suspended between night and day with our contrails etched across the frozen Arctic sky. It was one of the many gifts the airplane gave to me.

A CREW FINISHES

Nearly four years after we started the program, Walt and I had our final flight together. At the time, we didn't know it would be our last flight. It was one of those satisfying missions where everything worked out as planned and the jet flew flawlessly all day. We flew an operational sortie with a bonus at the end. After completing a long swing through Europe on a complex route, we were tasked to fly in an airshow in England upon our return. I felt a little like the Spitfire pilot of yesterday who left to do battle with the enemy, returned unscathed, and did a few low passes for the chaps back at the home field before landing. When we topped off with the last tanker, it was a good feeling to know that several thousand people were waiting to see us return. When we got out of the jet, that day in England, we shook hands and congratulated each other on a mission well-flown. Although the end was unforeseen, we couldn't have asked for a better finale than that.

Walt went to command an ROTC detachment; it was an excellent opportunity for him. I opted to stay at Beale to continue to instruct in the T-38 and schedule the remaining months of local SR-71 flights. We had experienced much, and lived moments we would remember for the rest of our lives.

Moments of contemplating the scene outside were rare, but long remembered. Frequently I issued prayers of thanks to Him who held us in safekeeping. I always figured prayers would reach heaven quicker from 80,000 feet.

CHAPTER V

Companion Trainer

Besides the SR-71, Beale Air Force Base was home to U-2 and TR-1 aircraft, KC-135Q tankers, and a small complement of T-38s. The T-38s served as a companion trainer for Beale pilots and a chase airplane for the SR-71. U-2 pilots, SR-71 crews and tanker copilots flew the T-38 in its companion trainer role. This enabled them to remain current in night and instrument flying in a cost-effective aircraft.

SR-71 crews enjoyed the T-38 because it meant flying without a space suit, having a canopy with a serious view, flying in a cockpit with simple instrumentation, and having no hostile threat below. Because the SR-71 was not able to turn tightly or maneuver freely, we enjoyed flying the T-38 just to do a loop, or go inverted, or to get our desire to maneuver out of our systems. The T-38 was a great little sports car of a jet. It was fun to let my RSO take the stick and try his hand at flying. Sitting in the backseat of the Sled wasn't much fun for him and a little romp in the blue in a '38 was good medicine. Walt became good with his flying even though he did perform a couple of maneuvers heretofore unseen.

PACE CHASE

A secondary mission for the Beale T-38s was to act as a chase aircraft for the SR-71. Airplanes flying a chase position provide assistance to another aircraft having an emergency. The chase pilot can help the pilot with the emergency by coordinating with Air Traffic Controllers, or helping with navigation. The T-38 could only provide this assistance to SRs flying near Beale. In some instances the T-38 provided valuable assistance to an SR-71, but most of the time it was never used for this.

Nevertheless, sorties were planned and flown to practice chasing the SR-71, so when the need arose, pilots had experience flying along side the airplane. These sorties were called Pace Chase. It was fun to go up in the T-38 and observe the SR-71 in flight. No matter how many times I flew the SR-71, I always had a sense of awe when I came up alongside it in a T-38. The size differential, the distinctive angular shape, and the way the big jet would bounce and flex in the turbulence always captured my attention. The Sled was always beautiful in flight.

T-38, the sports car of Beale.

Author climbs out from Beale in a T-38 on Pace Chase sortie. Minutes later the T-38 will join with the Sled.

Most pilots readily volunteered for Pace Chase sorties because it was exciting to fly formation with the Lady in Black. During my experiences, I was always amazed to see how the SR could easily out-accelerate the nimble T-38. I had to remember that when the SR was lightweight because of low fuel, it accelerated easily. While walking across base, I enjoyed looking up to see the Blackbird arcing overhead with a white sentinel close beside her.

High above the Sutter Buttes, a '38 chases a heavyweight Sled. Fuel is being dumped to reduce landing weight.

T-38 chases Blackbird through landing.

Author enjoys the freedom of movement in a T-38. There were no hostile threats observed over the Sierra Nevadas.

CHAPTER VI

On Display

I was fortunate enough to fly the Blackbird during a time when public displays of the airplane were more commonplace than were allowed in the early days of the program. The only thing we enjoyed more than flying her was showing her off to an enthusiastic crowd. People at airshows were genuinely excited to see the jet. It was a pleasure to talk with them and try to answer their questions.

I had attended many airshows before in other airplanes, but nothing compared to the attention the crowd gave the Blackbird. Even when the SR-71 didn't fly in the show, it seemed to be the main attraction. When it was scheduled to fly, no one left until it had flown. Most people had never seen the SR-71 before, so they were thrilled to see it on display and to talk with squadron members. Many were genuinely interested in everything about the SR-71 and they expressed appreciation for what we did that deeply touched us.

Some of the best airshows we attended were in England; the British really knew how to put on a show. Plenty of airplanes flew throughout the day, and at the larger airshows it was common for 150,000 people to attend each day of the event. When we displayed the Blackbird in England, it seemed as if every one of the 150,000 people wanted to see the jet up close. They wanted to talk to the crew members and have them sign their programs. We got writer's cramp, but we didn't complain; the people were such a joy.

Accurate data about the airplane was unavailable to the public for so long, many people filled in the blanks themselves. This made for some entertaining sessions while standing in front of the jet. Many times people were eager to show us how much they knew about our jet. We were interested in their estimates of the SR-71's performance; often they exceeded what the airplane was capable of doing. I'm not sure that we convinced some of them the SR-71 did not go into orbit during its missions. People knew we couldn't answer many of their questions, yet when their questions concerned classified information, they enjoyed hearing our answer, "I'm sorry, we can't talk about that." We noticed this response often generated more speculation on the topic. Even as the merits of different outrageous theories were discussed, people quickly assured us they understood we couldn't talk about some things, and they didn't want us to divulge any secrets to them.

SR-71 on display in England. The Brits knew how to throw an airshow.

Sometimes crews became tired after five or six hours of questions. I had to restrain a laugh one day as I heard a woman ask a simple question concerning the tires, only to get the can't-talk-about-it response from a weary crew member. Unfortunately for him, this started more fires than it put out. A small crowd, with new theories on the classified nature of rubber, gathered around the woman and asked even more questions.

Crowds enjoyed knowing some things about the airplane remained secret, and they were pleased to know that no one else had a plane like this. The shows we did in the United States were not as large as some others around the world, but no crowd anywhere in the world had more pride in this plane. Americans viewed the airplane as part of their heritage. It represented all that was strong about their country. The SR-71 had remained undefeated, undiluted, and number one for over twenty years. They often had even more regard for the airplane after talking to crew members.

The kids were the greatest, though. They not only wanted their programs signed, but also their hats and T-shirts. Even their hands became sites for our signatures. They weren't that interested in the Cold War, or intelligence gathering platforms, or stealth design. They wanted to know how fast they could go in that thing, and couldn't they just do it without the space suit, and just how many carrier landings have we made with this plane, anyway?

I really enjoyed talking to these young people because they reminded me so much of myself when I was their age. I remember inspecting jets at airshows in the 1950s, trying to understand why they didn't look exactly like their plastic likenesses I had recently built. Somewhere between watching the Blue Angels in their F-11s, and listening to the furious howl of an F-104, I became forever hooked on jets. My bicycle, in spirit, changed into everything from the Sabre Jet to the X-15. It was not unusual for me to think everyone knew what they wanted to do in life by the age of nine. I saw this same look on some of the young kids who gathered around our jet. I could tell by their questions that some of them were ready, and somewhere in that group stood a future aviator.

The SR-71 was a great airshow airplane because it was all the things people loved to see. It was fast, loud, and beautiful in a purposeful way. My fighter pilot friends frequently harassed me because my aircraft carried no gun, had one too many seats and couldn't maneuver. These were the same objections I had when I built the SR-71 model as a kid. I changed my opinion about the airplane, and they would too. Usually the same guys came back later and wanted their own personal tour of the jet.

Andrews AFB, 1958, where the author, on left, enjoys his first major airshow and forever loses his heart to the jets.

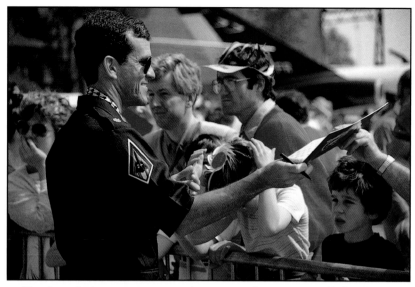

During airshows, crew members signed programs all day long.

Wherever we went, the SR-71 drew a crowd.

Sled pilot on display.

Flying the SR in front of thousands of people was a challenge. The jet, of course, wasn't designed for heavy maneuvering at low altitude. This mattered little, however, because the simplest maneuvers in this airplane were sure to please any crowd. Just flying straight and level and lighting the afterburners never failed to excite the people watching. The pilot's main problem was holding down the airspeed so he could turn around quickly for the next pass. A few simple passes that lasted only a few minutes required immense physical exertion from the pilot. This was one of the few times the backseater had nothing to do. After frequently telling Walt about the view he was missing while we were at altitude, he finally got back at me during an airshow by describing what a sight the large crowd was. Meanwhile, I was intently concentrating on aligning the aircraft for the next pass and watching the airspeed indicator.

The SR-71's most popular airshow demonstration was flying the jet through a maneuver we normally practiced in training to gain experience flying with one engine. We called this maneuver a simulated single engine go-around. One engine remained in idle and the other was pushed up to full afterburner. Because of the thrust differential, the aircraft would yaw greatly, putting the aircraft in a slight bank. It was perfect for shows; it was loud and the large deflection of the rudder and slight bank added flair. Since the wheels were down and only one burner was lit, speeds were easier to keep under control.

Airshow crowds' reactions varied while watching the different airplanes fly their demonstrations. Everyone loved watching the highly maneuverable F-16s. The World War II Spitfires and Mustangs were sentimental favorites. The Red Arrow's formation of nine jets with colored smoke evoked oohs and aahs. The SR-71 though, elicited a gaze of wonder from the crowd that was different than those caused by any other airplane. As the Sled passed overhead, the crowd would stare reverently at the jet and listen in awe as the unmistakable sound of full afterburner would echo across the airfield and back.

At the Dayton Air Fair, Walt and I found ourselves flying the SR-71 departure show. As we walked into the room our PSD folks were using for suit-up, we found ourselves surrounded by twenty to thirty newspaper and television reporters. We had to laugh to ourselves as we sat there in our longjohns being interviewed for the evening news.

We flew a couple of passes for the crowd and were about to head for home, when Walt received a call from the tower at nearby Wright-Patterson Air Force Base. They asked if we could make a pass by the Air Force Museum located across the main base. No one at the museum knew we were coming so there must have been some startled

SR-71 souvenirs were popular around the world. This collection was as good as any I had seen.

It is at airshows that future fighter pilots are born. This little guy had all the earmarks. Note ferocious logo on cap, stylish eye protection complete with jet blast restraint device, meaningful sized combat watch, clenched fist for effect, tall cool refreshment, serious airshow T-shirt, and the definite look of someone formulating a tactic to deal with one red rope.

folks on the ground as we thundered by the main entrance to the museum. As we rocketed upward in search of our tanker, our radio continued to crackle with the excited thanks of the tower. We finally had to ask him to leave our frequency because we needed it for the business at hand, but he made our day.

THE RARE SHOW

Normally, we landed the Sled at the same field from which we took off. We landed away only when the airplane had a serious problem or if the weather at the home base were bad enough to prevent a safe landing. When the jet got sick, our task became getting the plane down safely as soon as possible. Landing away was a big deal to everyone, from the people who used the film we brought back, to the people who maintained the airplane. We, in turn, depended on our support people to help us taxi in and shut down, to push the stands to the airplane, and help us unstrap and climb out. We needed help getting out of the space suit, and even the clothes we changed into hung in lockers at the PSD building back at Beale. Nearly every crew had at least one experience landing away and each one was an adventure. Walt and I landed away only one time, but the events of those few days were typical of what other crews encountered.

We had been up since one in the morning to prepare for an early takeoff from Beale to a target area in the Caribbean. We had flown nearly halfway across the United States when I realized we were losing oil pressure on the right engine. We were still climbing at 1500 knots and had not finished our accel to altitude. Walt quickly listed the fields suitable for landing along our route. These were not fields below us; instead they were 150 to 200 miles in front of us. This distance was needed to slow the jet and descend before we could fly our final approach to a landing at the chosen divert base. Peterson Field in Colorado was our destination. It was a joint use field, meaning that in addition to being an Air Force base, it also served as a municipal airport for Colorado Springs.

Most people had never seen an SR-71 unless they had attended an airshow with one on display. By the excited response we received from the air traffic controllers and airport personnel, we felt as if we were at an airshow instead of having an emergency. The tower gave us priority to land. The controller told a United flight its takeoff clearance was cancelled and it must hold for us. In my entire military flying career, this was the first time this had ever happened. The Sled performed bravely and we landed without incident.

An excited crowd watches crew prepare to fly the showstopper.

The simulated single engine pass, a crowd favorite at airshows. Large rudder deflection was necessary with one engine in idle and one in full afterburner.

A flurry of excitement greeted us on the ground. Every agency with a radio wanted to issue instructions or request our intentions. For a moment I felt like I was in complete control of the airport. If I had asked to taxi to the United terminal and have the Marine Band playing for us, someone would have made it happen. I finally told everyone to clear the frequency and informed them we would park on the military ramp. I inquired if there were any empty hangars, or ones that could be emptied immediately. There weren't. We ended up parking on the far end of the ramp, much like a normal military transient aircraft. As I taxied to our parking area, I noticed a crowd gathering along the road near the ramp.

During training, we had been thoroughly briefed on what actions to take if we had to shut down the engines without the assistance of ground personnel. Now that time was here, and we felt a little naked without the normal assistance of PSD and maintenance specialists. The landing away procedure required the RSO to unstrap himself, and with the engines still running, climb out of the aircraft. He would slide down the side of the plane and locate the landing gear safety pins, which were stored in an outer compartment of the airplane. The procedure of inserting them into the landing gear prevented inadvertent retraction of the wheels on the ground. After completing this step, the RSO signaled the pilot to shut down the engines, and monitored fuel venting as the engines spooled down. During this series of events performed by the RSO, the pilot sat in the cockpit with his feet on the brakes. I was glad I was the pilot.

Walt did a masterful job of locating and disconnecting all the straps and hoses holding him in the airplane. While he carefully stowed secret materials in the backseat, I noticed the crowd standing a few hundred feet away, had grown in size. The same look of wonder I had seen at airshows appeared on their faces. Walt told me he was ready to climb out of the airplane, and I thought how this maneuver was going to dazzle the crowd. Sure enough, the people stared in wonder as a space man popped out of the backseat, slid down the curved fuselage, and walked around underneath the jet. Many had the distinct look of people witnessing an alien landing.

Once I had shut down the plane and extracted myself, I noticed a blue staff car approaching. The base personnel helped us with our unusual requests. Security police were dispatched to guard the jet around the clock. We stored our classified materials in an appropriate facility. An airman was sent to Supply to pick up flight suits for us to wear. With instructions from us, base operations people helped us remove our space suits. Before we could even put on our new clothes, a Sergeant wanted to know when

Airshow delight — SR-71 in full afterburner overhead.

he could take his people in the weather facility out to the jet for a tour. The requests continued for two days. An entire maintenance team arrived from Beale to repair our plane. We were glad to see them arrive; their appearance was the first break we had from walking base officials around the jet. We enjoyed giving tours though, and were only sorry we had to show them a broken plane. This didn't seem to bother them at all.

Walt and I didn't know our takeoff time until maintenance gave us the word, but somehow everyone on base knew. They were there along the road, on the grass, and on the tops of buildings. I think half the people at the United terminal were watching too. The people at Peterson Field and Colorado Springs had treated us royally, and I knew they would enjoy seeing a flyby, but our standard departure procedure was simply taking off and climbing away quickly. Walt and I talked it over before suiting up. We thought it might be a good idea to check that darn oil system with a couple passes across the field, in case it went bad again. Heck, just to make sure, the smart thing would be lighting the afterburners while still at low altitude, and going to maximum thrust during a steep climb. With this plan, we'd know for sure the system was fixed.

On that beautiful afternoon in Colorado, so many people were thrilled with a simple oil system checkout pass.

The entire detachment poses at an airshow.

CHAPTER VII

The Legacy

Sometimes non-flyers can't understand the affection pilots feel for their planes. Everything we feel about the machine, we already have within ourselves. We bring the dreams, the joy, and the life to the plane when we enter the cockpit. We learn to feel as if we are one with the machine, and it becomes an extension of ourselves. Because the airplane holds our mortality in its hands, we love it for returning us safely. These feelings and the common experience we share with the airplane make its retirement difficult, no matter what airplane is retiring or what new exciting airplane is replacing it.

I have watched Air National Guard pilots take old Century Series fighters across the country to the boneyard at Davis-Monthan Air Force Base in Arizona. There, on the desert floor near the air base, they are stored in a dry environment that is kind to these metal machines. They may be used for spare parts or resurrected later as drones, but mostly they just sit in straight rows in the desert. Sometimes having stopped at an air base on a cross-country trip, I parked next to old planes I knew were on their way to Davis-Monthan. Like me, they had stopped for fuel on their trip across the country. Their faded paint was a clue of their imminent retirement. Another time I stood at Davis Monthan Base Operations and watched a pilot on this kind of ferry mission land his war-horse on a hot and windy afternoon. He slowly taxied to the ramp, where he shut the engines down for the last time. With sadness and reverence, he said a final goodbye in his own way and quietly left the hardened veteran to await its tow to the boneyard. Like a metal ghost from the past, the airplane sat alone in the quiet evening sunlight. In its frame of steel and wiring, it held untold stories of terrifying moments and other memories of sweet victory. Each jet I saw towed to its final desert parking spot looked proud. There, row upon row of airframes sit like silent sentinels. A harsh sun dulls their finish and weathers their insignia. Watching an airplane retire is as poignant as saying good-bye to a friend I know I will never see again.

Even though we knew the end of the SR-71 program was coming, it was no less sad living through that time when it finally arrived. The reasons for retiring the SR-71 were many. It was too expensive to operate. Satellites could do the job. The aircraft was getting old, and newer planes were going to be built to replace it. The list of reasons went on. We who had flown her, knew she was far from ready to leave. We also knew the program couldn't last forever. Though a few people fought to keep her, too many others understood little about her capabilities.

In 1989, the draw down of the program began in earnest, and aircraft were assigned for final disposition. Instead of the scrap heap, we were happy to learn most of the airplanes would rest intact, in air museums across the country. It was a sad time at Beale, watching the squadron of jets slowly deplete. One by one, they made their final takeoff from the runway they knew so well, to enjoy their final flight.

I was a scheduler during this time and coordinated the delivery schedule with some of the receiving agencies. The people I spoke with were eager to receive this addition to their collection of display aircraft. I couldn't share their joy or enthusiasm. The aircraft represented the genius, love and dedication of many people who worked with it since its inception. The SR looked far from ready to assume its new role in a museum. I imagined the airplane in a museum, and people walking by. They would stop to wonder about this mysterious aircraft. They wouldn't know about the experiences, the emotions, and the history the airplane holds. The jet will not tell them of the missions it flew, the MIGs it outran, the thunderstorms it crested, or the sweaty gloves it had gripping its stick during turbulent refuelings. Instead it will sit silently and, like all jets on display, it will keep its stories to itself. People visiting the museums will never hear the deafening roar of the J-58s, see the extended flame, or feel the sound against their bodies. As I thought these things, I knew I would never be able to see an SR-71 in a museum without always hearing it and feeling its sound touch me deep within my soul.

As I reviewed the list of airplanes slated for delivery, I recalled how each seemed to have a personality all its own. Like a list of old friends, their tail numbers brought to mind memories of times I had spent with each of them. Vivid pictures came to mind: colorful geography spread before me; an airshow where we flew the jet before 150,000 people; the speed, the incredible speed, that had been there when we needed it most; a quiet night alone with the stars; the violent moments of the unstarts; the delighted gaze of visitors as they observed a hangared Sled; the soft kiss of six tires on concrete after a long mission; the adrenaline on a night takeoff; the familiarity with gauges and levers, and the comfortable confines of the cockpit. The airplanes had become more than welded parts of titanium and steel to the men who had flown them. The Sled had propelled our lives to the very edge of all we held dear, and brought us back. Now we few who had flown this plane were a part of its history. Our moments with it were unique, forever a part of its silent past. As I reviewed the list on my desk, I felt proud and fortunate to have been a small part of the life of this airplane.

Crew awaits final start time before delivering a Blackbird to a museum.

The official retirement ceremony was anticlimactic, and for most, a bleak experience. Afterwards I felt as if I had attended the funeral of one still alive. For several more weeks, I scheduled SR-71s to leave for museums. Eventually the day came when the last one was scheduled for takeoff. I reminded myself that it was little more than a footnote to aviation history, but nonetheless, found myself driving out to the runway to observe the Sled's final departure. As I stood beside my vehicle and waited for the Blackbird to emerge from the hangar, I noticed only a few people had come out to watch the last plane leave Beale. Perhaps we had gotten too used to seeing it around the base. As I waited, I had a hard time imagining the base without the sight of the Blackbird overhead.

As the SR-71 taxied by, I knew I was witnessing the passing of an era. This era began with the fateful flight of Gary Powers in a U-2 and the resulting embarrassment to the Eisenhower administration. An order was issued to proceed with the development of a more advanced plane that couldn't be shot down. The SR-71 was the result. For three decades it performed its mission untouched by the other side. As it swung its long nose into the run-up area , the jet took on that proud look I had seen before.

I watched the support people scurry beneath the jet, carrying out their normal procedures. The familiar scene felt different because I watched with a heavy heart. The distinguished roar of the engines assaulted my hearing one more time, and I felt the jet defiantly telling all who could hear that it did not want to go away; it could still do the job. The airplane was still the best. The sound thundered across the airfield with the cry of one still undefeated, issuing its final challenge. When the run was completed and all the maintenance people had moved away, the jet sat alone, waiting to take the runway.

I saw her then as I had the very first time and tears welled in my eyes. I knew her better now and loved her more. How could I not love her, after all she had shown me? She had not changed, and she had not aged. She was a bit of the past and the future rolled into one, the hottest of hot rods, and a technological wonder built to last. As she sat there dripping fuel, leaning slightly forward on a sloped ramp, she embodied purpose and elegance. I knew I would always remember her that way, the elegant Lady in Black, superior in design and performance. Some people said that the continuous heating incurred at high speeds had caused the metals of the jet to weld tighter over the years, and she now flew faster than when she was new. I had flown her and I believed them.

I watched the last SR-71 pull two fiery plumes down the runway and climb steeply away, her voice echoing proudly across the foothills. My eyes strained to follow her,

The Sled hugs its own shadow at high noon as it performs its final engine run.

hoping somehow to keep her alive, but soon she was swallowed by a bright blue sky. Though the jet was miles away and out of sight, I could still hear the faint rumble of the J-58s.

I returned to the squadron when the sound of the Sled's engines could be heard no longer at Beale.

FINAL ROAR

On March 6, 1990, the SR-71 officially left the Air Force inventory with a final flight that would take the airplane to the National Air and Space Museum. Flying from Palmdale, California, to Washington D.C., the SR-71 left active duty with all the pride, performance, and dignity that marked every aspect of its 25 years of service. The SR-71 was retired with all of its speed and altitude records still unchallenged. En route to the museum, the jet set four new continental speed records. Total flight time from Los Angeles to Washington D.C. was 64 minutes. On its final day the Sled had averaged 2145 miles per hour.

Photography Notes

All the photographs in this book were taken by the author except for the following: p. 44, John Gaffney; and p. 29, U.S. Air Force photo.

The cameras used were the Nikon N2000, Nikon F3, and Nikon F4. A variety of lenses were used ranging from 20 mm to 400 mm. All the images were made from transparencies, using Kodachrome, Ektachrome, and Fujichrome film. Film speeds ranged from 25 ASA to 400 ASA.

The photographs were taken over a seven year period. Over 5000 slides were reviewed in the formation of this book. Whenever film was shot in England or Okinawa, it was refrigerated and transported back to the United States for processing.

Shooting the pictures was truly a labor of love and made for some unusual experiences. By far the most challenging were those images recorded from the cockpit of the SR-71 and the T-38. In the T-38, one to two cameras could be carried safely with the aid of special Velcro straps secured around my chest. The biggest difficulty lay in getting the guy in the other seat to fly the jet to the exact position from which the shot could be made. Invariably, there was an element of luck involved with this kind of aerial photography. I was not always scheduled to fly with another T-38, and when I was, the sun angles were often less than optimum. In these cases, the entire instrument panel would be reflected onto the canopy creating a distracting glare in the printed image. The weather itself was always unpredictable. Smoke and haze across the northern California foothills dulled many pictures. Although crew chiefs did their best to clean the canopy, I still shot through a thick, curved surface of plastic. I found shooting from the rear seat of the T-38 was normally better than shooting from the front cockpit. Because there was less curvature at the sides of the rear canopy, I could get the camera lens perpendicular to the plastic and achieve less distortion. Although it was cramped, with practice I could aim, focus, and shoot with some degree of stability.

The biggest advantage in the T-38 was having another pilot fly the plane while I peered through a viewfinder. Talking him into the best position was a challenge. His ability to put the jet in the best position was often the most critical factor in getting a good picture. When the schedule, the weather, and the position of the aircraft were perfect, the fate of the picture rested squarely with my ability to focus sharply under different bank angles, pitch attitudes, and g forces. On a typical day with a roll of 36 pictures, I might get two to four shots worth keeping. I was always assured of having a slight headache when it was over because looking sideways through a small opening in a camera while flying through a variety of maneuvers was uncomfortable.

Shooting from the cockpit of the SR-71 created some special problems. First, I couldn't put the camera to my eye because of the space helmet's face plate. This was not a problem for most outside shots, because the lens could be set to infinity to achieve perfect focus. Because I couldn't put the viewfinder to my face, I framed some shots poorly in the beginning, but I corrected this with practice. Second, I had to choose my shots carefully, because there was no opportunity to reload film. The 36 exposures were all I had. On one occasion, I solved this problem by taking two camera bodies, both loaded with a roll of film. I placed one in the large leg pocket of the space suit, and put the other on the right console. I never repeated this because of the delicate effort involved with changing the lens from one camera to the other. Wearing gloves made this tricky. If anything was dropped, it could not be retrieved from the floor until after landing.

Simply finding a place to store my camera in the cockpit was a challenge. I spent several hours sitting in the cockpit trying different combinations. Initially I tried stowing the camera in the leg pocket of the space suit, but found it almost impossible to retrieve when it had settled to the bottom of the pocket. I found the console to my right to be the best location after takeoff. Small knobs there created a channel in which the camera could rest. These knobs were used minimally throughout the flight and were not hindered by the camera's presence. Because of the minimal maneuvering experienced in the jet, the camera never fell from this place. Before takeoff, I stowed the camera in a pouch behind my left elbow, since the acceleration forces were too great for it to remain on the console unsecured. Once airborne and heading out to the tanker, I reached back, felt for the camera, and placed it out on the right console. Because I was unable to see it amidst the bulk of the space suit, I had to undo the Velcro and carefully pull the camera first up, and then out of the pouch. This bit of gymnastics had to be practiced several times on the ground before flight.

Both the camera and film were exposed to extreme temperatures within the cockpit environment. While resting on the console in flight, the camera became quite cold in an unheated cockpit pressurized to 25,000 feet. When I put it up on the front windshield area, it rapidly heated up from resting against the hot glass. I could only leave it there a couple minutes before the film suffered from the heat.

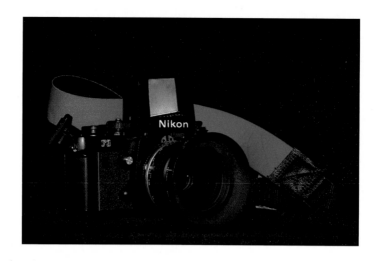

Like the Jet, my cameras had to be rugged and reliable
for use in the cockpit.

The self-portrait shots were the most difficult, and a great deal of film was expended to yield the few pictures I possess today. I premeasured the distance from my helmet to the windscreen while on the ground. I then set the camera to focus at this distance. By taking several shots I could make minor adjustments to this setting, hoping for one good one out of the bunch. I used the camera's auto-timer device, so I didn't have to reach up to snap the picture. Once I solved the focus, it was another chess game to produce the appropriate aperture. The constantly changing sun angles during turns in flight, and the extreme ratio of bright light to cockpit shadows, often defeated my attempts to produce a worthwhile image. In the end, it simply became a matter of how many attempts were made. The more I could shoot, the better the odds were for a lucky shot. This was not always easy. The basic business of flying the jet, precluded taking extra time to refine any one scene on film. Taking pictures was at the very bottom of my priority list of things to do in the cockpit. Many times the camera sat untouched throughout a flight. When I did reach for it, the picture taking was accomplished in a brief moment of rehearsed finesse. Shooting through the thick glass for the outside shots, I was always surprised at the clarity of some of the pictures.

Looking back over my collection of SR-71 pictures, there are few from the cockpit. I cherish these prized photos as I know how infrequently I was able to shoot them and how difficult it was to record the view as it really was. Safety of flight always came first, and I flew many hours in the jet before ever taking a camera along.

The pictures taken on the ground were only slightly less challenging. Once again, picture taking was only squeezed in while normally performing flight line duties. Over a long period of time, I slowly built the collection which helped me put this book together. I was fortunate to have many fine people provide opportunities for me to photograph these unique scenes. I never imagined when I entered the program that I would see the retirement of the SR-71, and I'm now so thankful I took the pictures I did.

FINAL NOTE

With the many thousands of SR-71 photographs I've taken, I am often asked which one is my favorite. It is an easy question to answer. To me, there was one among my collection which captured the essence of all that was mysterious and powerful about this jet. While flying on a tanker, I was able to get a picture of a Blackbird just prior to its refueling. Emerging from a squall line over the North Sea, the Sled dripped wet with rain and fuel as it moved slowly up toward my position in the boom pod. As we moved in and out of the clouds, I remember thinking what a powerful picture it would make if only there was more light. Like a wish granted, the bright rays of a partially hidden sun momentarily illuminated the Sled's wet metal and produced a satin-finished shine on the airplane I never again witnessed. It was the first time I had ever photographed the SR-71 in flight. Over the years, my photography improved, but I never captured another shot of the Sled more seductive to my eye. It now graces the cover of this book.

— Brian Shul —

Burner Climbs Daily ★ Airshows on Request
No Box Lunch ★ Meaningful MACH
Hostile Threats Met With Impunity

BRIAN SHUL
FIGHTER PILOT ★ SLED DRIVER

Attention Communists
For All You Do, This Boom's For You